A Way ot Escape

How to Handle the Tests and Temptations of Life

Valentine A. Rodney

For Conferences, Workshop, Crusades, Conventions and Seminars contact: Rev. Valentine Rodney
c/o Word Impact Ministries International
P.O. Box 787
Spanish Town
St. Catherine
Jamaica

Email: varodney@gmail.com
Tel: Jamaica: 876 390 2303 | USA : 407 545 5052

Published by:

Book Cover Design by: Iconence

ISBN: 978-1-958404-16-4 (paperback)
978-1-958404-19-5 (hardback)

First Edition: December 2022

Endorsements

It was in the year 1998. I was a young Christian going through a very trying time in my life. I listened to a pre-recorded message from a Youth Camp, which exposed me to a sermon detailing how to handle temptation by Rev. Valentine Rodney.

That which was a mountain in my life became a small hill. I learned how to live victoriously over temptation. I was both edified and empowered by that message then and recently on the morning devotion program. Applying those principles to my life has caused transformation and assisted in my spiritual formation.

I am extremely happy that this same message is now available in book form to reach countless individuals across the world struggling with that same giant of temptation. We can and must win the battle against temptation. Get it, get it, get it!

Minister Knox Murray
COGOP National Evangelism Director
Jamaica

Rev. Valentine Rodney is a gifted writer who possesses the anointing that leads him to compose books that speak directly and specifically to the reader. With that being said, I have no doubt that his latest book *A Way of Escape: How to Handle the Tests and Temptations of Life,* will truly minister to, transform, and bless your life.

This book is not a compilation of thoughts or opinions. It is written based on sound biblical principles that will challenge us through a series of self-examination exercises to discover the areas of our lives where we are vulnerable to temptation and how to safeguard said areas.

A Way of Escape: How to Handle the Tests and Temptations of Life is an excellent resource for all believers and can be likened to a Global Positioning System (GPS) as we navigate our Christian journey. While each corner is unknown to the traveler, an excellent GPS provides details on what lies ahead and the options that are available to circumvent upcoming dangers.

My prayer is that you not only read this book but that you allow it to invade your space. Yes, INVADE! Invasions often bring about destruction that results in change. May all the areas of your life that create temptation and manifest sin be utterly destroyed and that you experience change only

God can bring. Prepare yourself for a life-changing ride. It will be worth it!

INTERNATIONAL
WOMEN'S MINISTRY

Min. Moya Johnson Pugh
Sister 2 Sister International
Women's Ministry
Mulberry, FL

A *Way of Escape: How to Handle the Tests and Temptations of Life* is one of several books written by Rev. Valentine Rodney to assist believers in effectively navigating their way through life. This man of God was a special guest on the Facebook program *Morning Devotion,* and the teachings shared was responsible for the birthing of this book.

The teachings were enlightening, incisive, edifying, and motivational as many have attested to. What I found impactful was the fact that the teachings were grounded in the Word of God.

The teachings, especially on the significant stages of temptations, takes the believer on a journey that is clear, practical, and easily understood. I am confident that this book will be helpful to all believers in dealing with the tests and temptations of life.

I highly recommend this book to all and believe that it will strengthen, enlighten, and encourage you to persevere in your walk with God.

Owen Dwyer

Host: Morning Devotion

This book is unequivocally RIPE (Refreshing! Insightful! Practical! Empowering!) and is timeless in its application. Everyone who has been tempted and tested in some form or shape will find it extremely beneficial.

Rev. Valentine Rodney has a unique God-given gift to pull out practical biblical truths from God's Word and articulate it in a way that allows the reader to visualise, feel, and empathise with the plight, inner hurting and, sometimes, unspoken turmoil bubbling inside a Bible character's being. Not only will you be able to identify but also apply the concepts to your own life.

We have always heard to resist temptation; however, "A Way of Escape: How to Handle the Tests and Temptations of Life" will help strengthen your "spiritual resistance muscles" and help walk you through the "HOW" to achieve this.

Pastor: Triumphant Deliverance Centre

I am an avid reader of books, journals, and works of art that are geared towards self-improvement, expanding one's knowledge base, and bringing about long-lasting, effective changes in my life. I had the pleasure of reviewing this masterpiece, and it was as if the Lord told this author about my secret struggles. As Christians and believers in Christ, we are oftentimes bombarded with different opinions with no real biblical basis. This book, however, is the complete opposite, as it is sound in the scriptures and provides the reader with an opportunity to incorporate study points for later discourse.

The topics flow well and allow for easy reading. I must say that there were several moments where I had to pause and really review a few sentences due to the depth of the information being presented. There were several epiphanies and moments of real-life clarity that were quite evident as I scrolled through each page. If you are looking for a book that will not only challenge your way of thinking but also provide you with both practical and biblical solutions, then this work of art is for you.

The writing is informative, not opinion based, and the words flow from the heart of God, the Father, providing His children with the necessary tools and strategies to find our Way of Escape in this turbulent world. While the Way of Escape may not be smooth sailing or comfortable, this writer provides us with a timely reminder that the author of our lives is leading us, His children, along.

Dr. Renee Clarke APRN, DNP
President/Co-Founder
Dykal Health and Wellness

About the Author

 REV. VALENTINE A. RODNEY, BSc, MA. is an international speaker whose ministry has taken him to the USA, Canada, Europe, Africa, and several countries within the Caribbean, where he has also fostered and facilitated ministerial developmental programs. He has done undergraduate work at the University of the West Indies in Marine Biology and Graduate work in Missions at the Caribbean Graduate School of Theology.

Rev. Rodney has served in the areas of Christian Education, Evangelism, Leadership Development, Prayer and Intercession, Youth Ministry, Radio and Television, and Pastorate. He is also actively involved in welfare programs and mentorship to men, youths, and ministers. He is a strong advocate for Christian Transformational Development where the church interfaces with the community and assists in a strategic intervention that is both redemptive and empowering.

He is the author of the books "Shameless Persistence: The Audacity of Purposeful Praying," "The Power of the Secret Place: The Place of Relationship, Resolution, and Revelation," and "La Persistencia Desvergonzada: La

ix

Audacia de la Oración con Propósito." He has co-authored six other books with his friend and ministerial colleague, Rev. Nicholas "Robdon" Robertson. Rev. Rodney is the host and presenter of the television program *Word Impact* aired on MTMtv.

Rev. Rodney is an international instructor for Walk Thru The Bible Ministries, Co-Founder and Deputy Director for Impact Online Bible Institute (IOBI), Deputy Director of Build A Man Foundation, and the Director of Word Impact Ministries International, a non-denominational ministry that caters to the empowerment of the Christian Community and the salvation of the lost. He is an international Chaplain and Ambassador with Covenant International University and Seminary. His Motto is *"Go Where There Is No Path and Leave a Trail."*

REV. VALENTINE A. RODNEY is married to Yevett for over twenty-six years. Their union has produced two daughters, Zharia and Ana-Olivia.

Acknowledgments

There are so many persons that have contributed to my spiritual formation that the listing would be endless were names to be called, but I remain forever thankful.

Much thanks must be given to Owen Dwyer and Knox Murray, coupled with the morning devotion crew. This book, "A Way of Escape: How to Handle the Tests and Temptations of Life," would never have come to fruition without their insistence that what I was sharing on the Facebook program should be compiled. In fact, I was reminded by several persons about the impact that my message on temptation had on them several years ago.

It was that, coupled with the guidance of the Holy Spirit, that resulted in this work being done. So, for those who have anxiously waited, the time has come. I believe this book will surely be a blessing to the body of Christ and add value to the lives of countless others.

Foreword

It is always such a pleasure to read Rev. Valentine Rodney's book. Not only is he a master of enunciation, but every sentence in his book is a standalone revelation that can be harnessed as life-changing quotes for living and spiritual transformation. Only a divinely inspired writer can pen in such a matter, interlocking these powerful quotes into paragraphs and chapters to provide us with such a gem of a book that can be studied for ages.

This book, "A Way of Escape: How to Handle the Tests and Temptations of Life," packs a powerful punch in dealing with the issues analogous to all believers: tests and temptation. Some of the greatest spiritual leaders in the history of the church have fallen secretly to the inner promptings to violate God's law, and to say we are different and are not prone to the same propensities is a deception within itself. We are all flawed. This book will teach you how to transcend those flaws as help is available.

I pray that as you go through this revelatory book, your walk of faith will be deeply impacted, and you will be encouraged to rise up from your failures and never give up in trying to assimilate the Way of Escape that God provides when the tests and temptations emerge. Notice I said "when" and not "if."

C. Orville McLeish

Author of the Made in God's Image Series
Founder and CEO of HCP Book Publishing, God's Image
Jamaica, Impact One and God's Image Brand, and God's
Image Publications.

Contents

Introduction

What can I say about this book, but that it touches on some fundamental issues that are critical to the understanding of the Christian faith. Two of the most critical aspects of our faith deal with how we handle tests and temptations. The faith of many has been shipwrecked because of an inability to cope when faced with these two great challenges.

The book seeks to unearth what the scriptures clearly state concerning the subject matter and provide vital tips regarding overcoming or enduring. It gives a distinct view from God's perspective and so may provide a paradigm shift for some readers and a reinforcement for others.

The stand taken is not condemnatory but rather empowering. We will see a God who is concerned about the welfare of His people and has designed a way of escape. This book was born out of a need within the body of Christ for a handbook that would respond to some of the myriad of questions that are being asked by believers across the globe.

It addresses the issue of temptation, which affects both recent converts and those who have been in the faith for some time. Ignorance and resolve have hindered so many from being free from guilt and condemnation and thereby walking in the glorious liberty of Christ Jesus.

How to deal with anger and adversity coupled with the testing of our faith is covered. It is the expectation of the author that renewal and revival will take place as the concepts taught are applied.

Chapter 1

The Truth About Temptation

If you think you are standing strong, be careful not to fall. The temptations in your life are no different from what others experience. And God is faithful. He will not allow the temptation to be more than you can stand. When you are tempted, he will show you a way out so that you can endure. (1 Corinthians 10:12-13 – NLT).

"No man knows how bad he is until he has tried to be good. There is a silly idea about that good people don't know what temptation means" – C S Lewis

---

Whether you are a Christian or not, the challenge of succumbing to temptation is a constant reality. This pull to give in is a constant reminder of how frail and prone we are to doing wrong. The presence of temptation is a clear indication that we live in a world where standards exist. The pull or inducement to violate or to go against those standards is what constitutes temptation. The standards of which we speak are those set by God and entrenched in His Word. Thus, the result of falling to temptation is sin. Sin is referred to as all unrighteousness (see 1 John 5:17a), transgression of the law (see 1 John 3:4), missing the mark (see Romans 3:23, James 4:17), and hitting the wrong target (see Hebrews 10:26).

What is Temptation?

- An evil incentive.
- Coaxing, manipulating, or inducing a person into committing a sinful act.
- An enticement to do wrong through the promise of pleasure or gain.
- A strong urge or desire to disobey God and His Word.
- To put to the test.
- An enticement to sin, whether arising from one's desires or from outward circumstances.

Temptation is the reason why we are moved and motivated to sin. Before every sin comes an invitation called temptation. Temptation in and of itself is not sin; we sin by giving in to temptation.

Temptation is not Sin

Jesus, the Son of God, knew what it was to be tempted, but He never sinned. The Spirit of God led Him into the wilderness; however, it was Satan who tempted Jesus.

Then Jesus was led by the Spirit into the wilderness to be tempted there by the devil. (Matthew 4:1 – NLT).

20

It is important for us to understand why God's Spirit led Jesus into the wilderness to be tempted. We know that Jesus was fully God and fully man, but how would His humanity respond in a time of temptation? It is clear from the scriptures that He did not yield or give in but submitted Himself to the will of God. By His resistance, He overcame temptation and sin to give us the assurance that He would save or rescue those who are tempted.

For this reason he had to be made like them, fully human in every way, in order that he might become a merciful and faithful high priest in service to God, and that he might make atonement for the sins of the people. Because he himself suffered when he was tempted, he is able to help those who are being tempted. (Hebrews 2:17-18 – NIV).

Like Jesus, our trust, dependence, and reliance on God will give us victory in overcoming the tests and temptations of life.

During the days of Jesus' life on earth, he offered up prayers and petitions with fervent cries and tears to the one who could save him from death, and he was heard because of his reverent submission. (Hebrews 5:7 - NIV).

The Source of Temptation

God will test but never tempt us. God's testing is designed to both build character and cause us to truly depend upon Him. The test will clearly demonstrate both our obedience and love for Him. The testing will develop the qualities of patience and endurance in the life of the believer. Our unwillingness to surrender in times of temptation or testing will prove our unwavering and unswerving love and loyalty to God.

Dear brothers and sisters, when troubles of any kind come your way, consider it an opportunity for great joy. For you know that when your faith is tested, your endurance has a chance to grow. So let it grow, for when your endurance is fully developed, you will be perfect and complete, needing nothing. (James 1:2-4 - NLT).

We bring much honour and glory to God through being victorious in the tests, trials, and temptations that we face in this life. This is especially true when we do not wilt under pressure but are faithful in our service and devotion to Him. However, there should be much reluctance on our part in testing or tempting God through wilful acts of disobedience or endeavouring to find fault with His guidance and will.

The internal aspect of temptation is based on our own desires, while, externally, it deals with the provocation of tests and trials. The internal temptations are based on our sinful nature and its proclivities which are aimed, if we yield, to destroy us. The external temptations, as allowed by God, are building blocks for our spirituality, for example, Satan's tempting of Job. The character-building is achieved by those who endure or persevere when being tried. God is not trying to destroy us; He is intent on building us.

God blesses those who patiently endure testing and temptation. Afterward they will receive the crown of life that God has promised to those who love him. (James 1:12 - NLT).

Temptation will minimise the real negative danger or consequences of our decision-making while maximising the imagined positive benefits. Internal temptations and some external ones come in a verbal form trying to induce us to act. When we resist temptation, we are delivered from its consequences and are rewarded with the satisfaction that through Christ Jesus, we have overcome.

The desire to sin by man in the Garden of Eden came through three distinct aspects: the lust of the flesh—tree was good for food, lust of the eyes—pleasant to the eyes, pride of life—a thing to be desired to make one wise. We must accept responsibility and the consequences for the choices we make that contravene the instructions of God to us.

What is causing the quarrels and fights among you? Don't they come from the evil desires at war within you? You want what you don't have, so you scheme and kill to get it. You are jealous of what others have, but you can't get it, so you fight and wage war to take it away from them. Yet you don't have what you want because you don't ask God for it. (James 4:1-2 - NLT).

Caution Against Overconfidence

While we remain confident and steadfast as Christians, we must never rely simply on our own abilities to overcome. Trusting completely in God will result in fewer casualties. Overconfidence is always rooted in the issue of pride. Pride is an over-high opinion of oneself that makes us vulnerable through arrogance to carelessness in decision-making. Temptation operates like rocks in the harbour. At low tide, it is easily seen and can be avoided, but as the tide rises, it may not be discernible until you crash against it. The person who thinks he stands will not guard against temptation and so easily falls prey to it. We must resist the temptation to be selfish and self-focused based on our vulnerabilities.

Pride goes before destruction, and haughtiness before a fall. (Proverbs 16:18 - NLT).

It is important to recognise our areas of weakness and to always exert vigilance. Let us be aware and honest in acknowledging where we are more prone to err and put in place the necessary safeguards. Jesus' admonition is a necessary safeguard.

Keep watch and pray, so that you will not give in to temptation. For the spirit is willing, but the body is weak! (Matthew 26:41 - NLT).

With regard to temptation, it is important to note that God has the ability to deliver.

So you see, the Lord knows how to rescue godly people from their trials, even while keeping the wicked under punishment until the day of final judgment. (2 Peter 2:9 - NLT).

Temptation Seeks to Lay Hold of You

The temptations that we face are indeed active and work to seize and hold us fast, attempting to make us bow to its influence. Before every sin lies a temptation. If we defeat the temptation, we will not commit the sin. It is amazing that once you give in to temptation, it no longer exists, but you will feel drained and defeated.

It is important in facing temptations not to consider our situations unique or an exception to the norm. Many persons have faced similar or worse temptations and, through the enablement of God, have found the strength to overcome. The lie of the enemy is to make us feel that no one has ever had it as hard as we do. God, however, reminds us that our temptations are never unique. What holds us in bondage to sin is believing the lies about our temptations. The truth that you believe and apply to your life is liberating.

And you will know the truth, and the truth will set you free. (John 8:32 - NLT).

Lies About Temptation

1. The devil made me do it.
2. The Spirit of God should have warned me.

25

3. It's God's fault. He knew I was weak.
4. This was more than my ability to endure.
5. It was too strong, and I could not help myself.
6. I can't stop myself; it is too late for me.
7. I am not perfect.
8. Praying does not help.

Let us bear in mind that it is possible to resist all temptations through the power of the Holy Spirit. Once the deception of the temptation comes to light and is exposed, it will lose its power. The most important word to use during your temptation is "No." The truth of God's Word is both empowering and liberating.

God Will Govern the Extent of Our Temptation

Whenever we are tempted, there needs to be total and complete reliance on God's faithfulness. He will provide help in every temptation, and this help is readily and easily accessible. Our reaction to temptation will be dependent on our individual weaknesses. Rest assured that God will allow the Holy spirit to act as a governor so that we will be able to manage. The temptations are limited based on our ability to rely upon Him for help. We will never handle temptations through self-reliance.

The power of temptation is limited to less than our ability to endure and not sin. Our strength may not increase, but we are being supervised during the test. We can always cry out for help as needed. The situations may vary, but our God remains the same. As we grow in God and mature, we gain confidence and insight into how to embrace the help God offers on how to handle temptations.

A Way of Escape

This is the greatest news ever, that God will show us an escape route during our temptation. Temptations always come with this safety outlet. He will provide the way of escape but will not force us to use it. This is a decision we must make as the way is revealed or provided. This is not a temporary relief from the pressure associated with giving in, but rather being able to stand up to it despite its repeated advances.

Barclay says the word for **a way of escape** is really *a mountain pass*, with the idea of an army being surrounded by the enemy, and then suddenly seeing an escape route to safety. Like a mountain pass, the **way of escape** is not necessarily an easy way out, but it is made available.

Being tempted is not a sin. The major problem is either entertaining the temptation or surrendering to it. We do not need to accept the condemnation of the enemy when we are being tempted; we just need to find ways not to give in. The way of escape has been provided by God so that we might be able to bear the temptation. It is therefore important that we recognise the strength God provides through the Holy Spirt as we engage in prayerful vigilance.

Keep watch and pray, so that you will not give in to temptation. For the spirit is willing, but the body is weak." (*Mark 14:38 - NLT*).

There is a need for all believers to stay alert and to be on guard against the possible attacks of the enemy. We are faced with similar tests and temptations, but we need to stand our ground in faith as we continuously look to God for strength and support.

Stay alert! Watch out for your great enemy, the devil. He prowls around like a roaring lion, looking for someone to devour. Stand firm against him, and be strong in your faith. Remember that your family of believers all over the world is going through the same kind of suffering you are. (1 Peter 5:8-9 - NLT).

We are much stronger when we come together in prayerful support and mutual accountability. The community of believers is there to provide comfort, consolation, and hope even as we all repose ourselves in the fact that God will never abandon us in our time of need.

Chapter 2

The Six Stages of Temptation

God blesses those who patiently endure testing and temptation. Afterward they will receive the crown of life that God has promised to those who love him. And remember, when you are being tempted, do not say, "God is tempting me." God is never tempted to do wrong, and he never tempts anyone else. Temptation comes from our own desires, which entice us and drag us away. These desires give birth to sinful actions. And when sin is allowed to grow, it gives birth to death. (James 1:12-15 - NLT).

The holy man is not one who cannot sin—a holy man is one who will not sin.

To break free from the clutches of temptation, it is important to understand how it works so a plan of action can be developed. The intended outcome of temptation is to cause us to sin. Our relationship with God plays a key role in how we deal with temptations. Our love for God and the intimacy we share with Him should propel us away from yielding to the desire to sin.

When is it easier to yield to temptation?

1. Physically tired.
2. Emotionally drained.
3. Mentally discontented.
4. Spiritually burnt out.
5. Relationally bankrupt.
6. Insecure.
7. Angry.
8. Deeply offended.

No one is exempt from being tempted. Spiritual maturity may cause temptation to be more manageable, but it will not prevent us from being tempted. It is unacceptable to believe that God is responsible for our temptation. We must avoid seeking someone to blame for our sinning because of temptation.

In the Old Testament narrative with Adam and Eve (see Genesis 2:15-3:7), the command of God was clear concerning the two trees in the garden. They could eat from every tree except the one in the midst referred to as the tree of the knowledge of good and evil. The tree was not placed in the garden for evil solicitation but to test man's loyalty, love, and commitment to God. Any choice or decision to disobey or doubt God will always be deemed as evil.

The serpent raised two fundamental questions that caused Eve to doubt God: What did God say concerning eating from every tree, and what is God hiding from you (you shall not surely die, but your eyes shall be opened, and you shall be like a God). She fell victim to the lust of the flesh, the lust of the eyes, and the pride of life (see Genesis 3:6).

The result was that Adam blamed God by saying, "the woman You gave me" (see Genesis 3:12), and the woman blamed the serpent that he deceived her (see Genesis 3:13). The issue with temptation is that once we become its victim, we tend to find someone to blame rather than accepting personal responsibility for our actions. Since God is behind all creation, it is easy to blame Him for our misfortunes. We might believe that God allowed for the fall and failure than to consider that a clear principle had been violated, evidenced by the disobedience.

The pressure to do evil is never from God. God will never put evil in our way. Yielding to temptation is never God's will for our lives. We need to stop attacking God when we are tempted and start soliciting His help to save or rescue us. When we examine God's character and motive, He has no evil intentions toward us. The scriptures contain solid advice with regard to how temptations work and how to overcome. Let us submit both to the sovereignty of God and the Word of God.

God allows temptation, but He does not tempt us. God will never entice us to do evil. He will test our faith without soliciting us to do evil. Rest assured, God cannot be tempted to do evil. From the perspective of God, we are faced with a trial or a test, but from the enemies' side, we are faced with a temptation. It is out of the trials that the temptations come.

Let us not transfer the work of the enemy and attribute that to God.

It is commonly stated that *"Opportunity knocks once, but temptation beats on the door every day."* It is not the bait that is the sin but the bite.

Several distinct stages of temptation have been identified, showing how it works to cause us to fail/fall by sinning against God.

Stages of Temptation

Stage 1: Desire (Lusts)

It is clear from the passage that temptation comes from our own desires. In the original creation of man, he was built with Godly desires to share both communion and communication with God and, by extension, have proper interpersonal relationships. This purity, however, was marred through the introduction of sin. Desire was corrupted by man's wilful act of disobedience to God. The result is a fallen nature that is actively in rebellion against God.

Thus, temptation comes when our desires begin to trump God's expectations for our lives. In many instances, it is a desire for what is expressly forbidden by God as revealed through His Word.

It is important that we identify the:

- Person who tempts us.
- Situation that tempts us.
- Activity that tempts us.
- Place that tempts us.
- Thoughts that tempt us.

Rather than entertaining the thought, we need to shift focus and think about something else. We encourage temptation to the extent that we dwell on unholy thoughts and desires. We must fill our minds with wholesome thoughts to weaken our resolve to become prey to evil desires.

And now, dear brothers and sisters, one final thing. Fix your thoughts on what is true, and honorable, and right, and pure, and lovely, and admirable. Think about things that are excellent and worthy of praise. (Philippians 4:8 - NLT).

We need to guard our hearts against the desire to find fulfilment in areas that the scriptures and the Holy Spirit clearly indicate are off-limits. It is important that we regularly do a heart check to see what we are entertaining or are allowing entrance. *"An ounce of prevention is better than a pound of cure."*

Guard your heart above all else, for it determines the course of your life. (Proverbs 4:23 - NLT).

What is in your heart determines the pull. Examine yourself to see whether there is a sensual, covetous, unforgiving, or hardened heart. We must be honest with ourselves and not ignore the warning signs.

33

We would do well to consider the admonition of Apostle James with specific reference to how our lusts can result in serious relationship casualties while simultaneously destroying us.

What is causing the quarrels and fights among you? Don't they come from the evil desires at war within you? You want what you don't have, so you scheme and kill to get it. You are jealous of what others have, but you can't get it, so you fight and wage war to take it away from them. Yet you don't have what you want because you don't ask God for it. And even when you ask, you don't get it because your motives are all wrong—you want only what will give you pleasure. (James 4:1-3 - NLT).

Stage 2: Deception (Drawn Away and Enticed)

What catches our attention can throw us off-guard to the extent that we lose our focus on what really should be a priority. This concept can be used as a metaphor to indicate the interest shown by a fish based on the allure of the bait. Once the bait is seen, it goes after it with one intention to have it. It could also be used of a harlot drawing a young man out of the right way with the promise of pleasure. This unique feature of temptation pulls you from behind the barriers of self-restraint through repeated offerings. To be drawn away is to be drawn into temptation. Remember always that temptation is an evil solicitation.

It is often stated that it is the second and third look that begins the cycle of entanglement. The purpose therefore is to pull us away from God's intended purpose for our life. We are pulled based on the promise that we envision and the expectations we have. We move from safety to risky the longer we allow ourselves to be preoccupied in our thoughts by what we have seen. Enticement seeks to weaken our will and resolve, making the temptation more appealing/alluring. This is intended to pressure us towards succumbing to the temptation. At this stage we are thinking, processing, and considering our next move.

In some instances, we give Satan too much credit for his tempting powers, not recognising that our desires play an integral role. Our attitude often reflects carelessness or naivety on our part, almost like we are begging the enemy to tempt us. The scriptures caution us against falling to the evil enticement of the enemy to sin through promises that are made. Jesus demonstrated how to overcome this enticement (lure) in His confrontation with Satan in the wilderness. He consistently referred to the standard of the Word of God and refused to be drawn into participating in the enemy's request.

During that time the devil came and said to him, "If you are the Son of God, tell these stones to become loaves of bread." But Jesus told him, "No! The Scriptures say, 'People do not live by bread alone, but by every word that comes from the mouth of God.'" Then the devil took him to the holy city, Jerusalem, to the highest point of the Temple, and said, "If

*you are the Son of God, jump off! For the Scriptures say,
'He will order his angels to protect you. And they will hold
you up with their hands so you won't even hurt your foot on
a stone.'" Jesus responded, "The Scriptures also say, 'You
must not test the LORD your God.'" Next the devil took him
to the peak of a very high mountain and showed him all the
kingdoms of the world and their glory. "I will give it all to
you," he said, "if you will kneel down and worship
me." "Get out of here, Satan," Jesus told him. "For the
Scriptures say, 'You must worship the LORD your God and
serve only him.'" (Matthew 4:3-10 – NLT).*

We should also consider at this stage moving away from the
source of enticement or stop the train of thoughts heading in
the wrong direction and re-focus. When it comes to external
temptation, run or resist, and regarding internal temptation,
simply stop trying to convince yourself that it is okay.

Stage Three: Conception *"When Desire is Conceived"*

This implies that we have been seized and made a prisoner
to our sinful desires. There is now a strong need to fulfil
what is on the inside. The desire has grown sufficiently to
the point where you want to cave in and respond to the
pressures. It has taken root and claimed us. The decision to
sin is now foremost in our mind. This conception is going to
affect us emotionally (feelings), mentally (thought life), and
volitionally (will to choose).

In conception, we move from desire to defending our desires and then ultimately to deciding to fulfil the desire and sin. Many will agree that initially, there is a strong desire to commit the sin, then you start to think of reasons why you should (justification), and then finally plan carefully how to get away with the sin. At this stage, the benefits appear to far outweigh the consequences.

However, we have not reached the point of no return. We can abort this conception by using the truth of the scriptures. There is the need to pull back and not entertain this anymore. Stop convincing or giving yourself a good reason to sin. The struggle at this stage is intense but not insurmountable. Why not share with an accountability partner what you are going through and devote some time to counsel, prayer, and the Word?

Stage 4: The Birth "It Gives Birth to Sin"

There is always a period between conception and birth that provides an opportunity to change our minds and forego the sin. The Holy Spirit will often provide this opportunity as a way of escape so that we do not become victims to the temptation. It is the responsibility of the Holy Spirit to convict us of our evil intentions and desires. He will mercifully and graciously plead with us so we can avert the impending disaster. If we submit to the conviction, we would have saved ourselves before it was too late.

If we resist the Holy Spirit, then the plan to sin will be executed. But all too often, after the short-lived pleasure and euphoria, comes the startling realisation of what we have done. In some cases, there is guilt, embarrassment, regret, and a sense of deadness of having failed miserably. In other cases, there is just this resignation that we could not have done any better. Sometimes there is shock and a fear with regard to how this will affect our reputation and life.

It is important that we recognise this does not have to be the end; we can still recover and rebound. Let us heed the admonition of John, the Apostle, and be reconciled to God.

My dear children, I am writing this to you so that you will not sin. But if anyone does sin, we have an advocate who pleads our case before the Father. He is Jesus Christ, the one who is truly righteous. He himself is the sacrifice that atones for our sins—and not only our sins but the sins of all the world. (1 John 2:1-2 - NLT).

Stage 5: The Growth "And Sin, When Full Grown"

Whenever we continue to give in to sinning, it will keep growing and expanding. With each act of sinning, it becomes easier to move on to the next. Sin is never satisfied with the same level and will quickly degenerate into something worse. Sin is never satisfied until it rules and controls our lives.

Every sin we commit is digging a spiritual grave that will lead to total apathy if not stopped. At this stage, it appears that everything is spiralling out of control, and we are powerless to stop it. How often do we weep, beg for forgiveness but go back to sinning? We feel trapped and hopeless, wondering if this will ever end. We need to stop telling ourselves it is the last time and turn to God and truly mean it. Many of us who are trying to cope can testify that each time we sin, it becomes easier to give in and harder to resist, but we can overcome this defeated lifestyle by turning to God with our whole heart.

If we claim we have no sin, we are only fooling ourselves and not living in the truth. But if we confess our sins to him, he is faithful and just to forgive us our sins and to cleanse us from all wickedness. (1 John 1:8-9 - NLT).

Stage 6: The Death *"Brings Forth Death"*

With repeated sinning, the power of sin becomes greater in our lives. We now sin with practiced ease, and it becomes more difficult to stop. Despite our prayers and self-will, we find ourselves sinking deeper and deeper. Succumbing to sin will only cause it to dominate our lives

Obedience to God leads to life and victory, while disobedience leads to sin and death. Death will lead to doubting everything about God's ability to help us and our salvation through Christ. We may become depressed and show hostility to the scriptures and those who represent Christ.

Practicing sin leads to both bondage and enslavement. It becomes difficult to see and embrace truth because of the sin. The addiction to sin now brings a sense of despair, hopelessness, and helplessness. We may so despair of hope that we feel we are beyond the scope of God's grace, sinking from one level of depravity to the next. We are now blinded to both the consequences of sin and the truth of God's Word to deliver.

We can feel the effects of the broken fellowship and the widening distance between ourselves and God. We have become mortally wounded and cannot save ourselves, but God is still merciful and forgiving. He has the authority to break the power of sin over our lives.

God's law was given so that all people could see how sinful they were. But as people sinned more and more, God's wonderful grace became more abundant. So just as sin ruled over all people and brought them to death, now God's wonderful grace rules instead, giving us right standing with God and resulting in eternal life through Jesus Christ our Lord. (Romans 5:20-21 - NLT).

The answer is found in Jesus. He will raise us up from spiritual death to life. Christ came to redeem us from sin, self, and Satan through the offering up of Himself to God as the price for our transgressions. We, therefore, embrace the following and commit to walking in our freedom:

- Sin shall no longer reign or have authority over us (see Romans 6:12).

- We will not give ourselves over to sinful proclivities and lifestyles (see Romans 6:13).
- Sin is no longer our master (see Romans 6:14).
- We have now surrendered our hearts and lives to obey God (see Romans 6:16).
- Our allegiance to Christ now frees us from being slaves to sin (see Romans 6:17).
- We are now free by God's grace to serve Christ wholeheartedly (see Romans 6:18).
- Our bodies have now become predisposed to righteousness and holy living (see Romans 6:19).

Let us be encouraged. The very life of Christ is now operating through us, and we no longer operate under the bondage of guilt and condemnation.

So now there is no condemnation for those who belong to Christ Jesus. And because you belong to him, the power of the life-giving Spirit has freed you from the power of sin that leads to death. (Romans 8:1-2 - NLT).

We give God thanks always for what He has done and stand in the deliverance that He affords. We, through Christ Jesus, are now declared free.

For he has rescued us from the kingdom of darkness and transferred us into the Kingdom of his dear Son, who purchased our freedom and forgave our sins. (Colossians 1:13-14 - NLT).

Chapter 3

The Good of Affliction

Before I was afflicted I went astray, but now I obey your word. You are good, and what you do is good; teach me your decrees. Though the arrogant have smeared me with lies, I keep your precepts with all my heart. Their hearts are callous and unfeeling, but I delight in your law. It was good for me to be afflicted so that I might learn your decrees. (Psalm 119:67-71 - NIV).

The task of the preacher is to comfort the afflicted and afflict the comfortable. – Vance Havner

---

In most cases, affliction is viewed in a negative light and having no positive benefits. Merriam-Webster describes affliction as a cause of persistent pain and distress; the state of being afflicted by something that causes great suffering. Most times, the focus on affliction is based primarily on how you feel and when will it end.

The struggle sometimes with affliction is trying to determine whether you did something to deserve it. Is this payback for a sin or atrocity committed? Could this be because of spiritual warfare? Am I under a generational curse? The list of causative factors is long and exhaustive. One thing we can all agree on is that affliction causes pain, undue pressures, stress and, in some cases, many anxious moments.

Afflictions can result in not just physical pains and bodily discomforts, but also serious mental agony and distress. This can be attributed to the effects of sickness, poverty, oppression, perverted justice, and a plethora of life-humbling situations. In considering the question of affliction we need to decide concerning our comfort and God's purpose.

Dear friends, don't be surprised at the fiery trials you are going through, as if something strange were happening to you. Instead, be very glad—for these trials make you partners with Christ in his suffering, so that you will have the wonderful joy of seeing his glory when it is revealed to all the world. If you are insulted because you bear the name of Christ, you will be blessed, for the glorious Spirit of God rests upon you. If you suffer, however, it must not be for murder, stealing, making trouble, or prying into other people's affairs. But it is no shame to suffer for being a Christian. Praise God for the privilege of being called by his name! (1 Peter 4:12-16 - NLT).

The Necessity of Afflictions

1. Broadens our spiritual perspective with respect to the ways of God.

2. Disciplines us in our walk with God.
3. Exposes deep-rooted attitudes and beliefs that rise to the surface under pressure.
4. Reveals our hearts and leads to a greater dependence on God.
5. Strengthens our faith in God.
6. Furnishes and equips us to handle greater difficulties in life.
7. Purges so that we become more fruitful.

The experiences obtained during affliction become a great teacher. We garner much wisdom from what we have been through and are capable of better decision-making under adverse conditions. There is always a truth to be learned through adversity. Not much is learned without affliction. We learn how to reconcile God's love for us and the fiery furnace of afflictions that we pass through. To be sure, no one is exempt from afflictions. Afflictions are not reserved only for the ungodly and unrighteous. The Godly and penitent have their fair share.

The righteous person faces many troubles, but the LORD comes to the rescue each time. (Psalm 34:19 - NLT).

We may not be spared the onslaught of troubles, but we have the assurances of either deliverance or endurance during those trying times. Note that it is God's responsibility to deliver us. Our deliverance hinges heavily on our obedience to Him. Even though He knows what we are experiencing, we are still obligated to persistently call upon Him.

Let us be comforted in the certain knowledge that God has not left us alone during trying times.

And we know that God causes everything to work together for the good of those who love God and are called according to his purpose for them. (Romans 8:28 - NLT).

The Intent of Affliction

Affliction is designed to drive us to the Lord. It is an important signal to alert us when our lives have veered off course. There is nothing like affliction to remind us of the direction that we should take. Before I was afflicted, I went astray (see Psalm 119:67).

God will use affliction as a means of getting our attention. With the onset of trouble, it is important that we turn to God for help. It is in turning to God that we can make sense of our crisis.

When I was in deep trouble, I searched for the Lord. (Psalm 77:2a - NLT).

When God spoke to Manasseh and His people, they would not listen. It was captivity that made them humble themselves and call, which led to their restoration (see 2 Chronicles 33:10-12).

Contrary to popular belief, affliction is evidence of God's faithfulness. He knows that this will cause us to turn or return to Him as we seek reconciliation. We can shorten the season of our affliction through our obedience to God.

Like the children of Israel, affliction will birth a cry in our hearts for deliverance by God. God has both our deliverance and deliverer on schedule. God is more interested in delivering than leaving us.

Years passed, and the king of Egypt died. But the Israelites continued to groan under their burden of slavery. They cried out for help, and their cry rose up to God. God heard their groaning, and he remembered his covenant promise to Abraham, Isaac, and Jacob. He looked down on the people of Israel and knew it was time to act. (Exodus 2:23-25 - NLT).

We must learn! The primary purpose of affliction is not to test us but to teach us how to walk right and live holy before God. When we understand God's role in affliction, it will take the pressure off us.

We should never allow outer turmoil to affect our inner peace. It is important that we develop a love for correction and instruction. When we are teachable and trainable, it augers well for our walk with God.

Our strongest point of reference and support during affliction is the Word of God.

God's discipline during affliction must bring us back to Him. The principles of the scriptures will serve as our

47

guiding light. The Word is there to bring order and stability to our lives. It is important that we develop a healthy appetite for God's Word. The Word will reveal God's standards and set boundaries for our living.

Afflictions often get worse before deliverance comes. It is important that we learn to bear up under the pressure and never give up on God. Exodus 4:29-31 reveals that with the promise of deliverance came increased burdens, unbearable bondages and beatings, and the demands to still function despite the provision of less resources. The enemy will intensify temptations, influence people against us, use lies and deception to undermine our character and integrity, and try to send us on guilt trips to make that period of our lives unbearable. We need to remember and understand that God will never let us down. Our attitude towards suffering is important. We should never hate the message of deliverance because of our sufferings, but rather it should foster greater communion and trust in God.

Good of Affliction

The real purpose of affliction is always manifested through the pains that we experience. We will ultimately recognise that all evil designs and intent will be overruled by good in the end. Our personal lives will benefit from a greater understanding of our God. The experience will make us better and not bitter. It is possible for us to experience a greater proximity to God despite the challenging times. Our receiving God's help during those testing times will result in us recognising that our suffering is not in vain.

Yet what we suffer now is nothing compared to the glory he will reveal to us later. (Romans 8:18 - NLT).

The disturbances and upheavals of the affliction will propel us toward our divine destiny. Because of the experience garnered, we would have learned to wise up and make better decisions. Afflictions not only give us a unique perspective on life and God, but it aids in our spiritual formation and character development. It is said that prosperity may blind, but adversity opens our eyes.

Chapter 4

Prescription for Dealing With Anger

Do not be quickly provoked in your spirit, for anger resides in the lap of fools. (Ecclesiastes 7:9 - NIV).

You cannot see your reflection in boiling water. Similarly, you cannot see truth in a state of anger. – unknown

---

Anger is normally interpreted as a response to a threat whether real or perceived. It is a strong feeling of displeasure usually aroused by a wrong—a strong feeling or emotion that makes you want to hurt someone or be unpleasant, a strong feeling of annoyance, displeasure, or hostility.

Anger is a way to express negative feelings, or it becomes a motivation to find solutions to problems. It is a strong emotional reaction of displeasure, often leading to plans for revenge or punishment.

The Bible on Anger

- People with understanding control their anger; a hot temper shows great foolishness. (Proverbs 14:29 – NLT).

- And "don't sin by letting anger control you." Don't let the sun go down while you are still angry. (Ephesians 4:26 - NLT).

- Understand this, my dear brothers and sisters: You must all be quick to listen, slow to speak, and slow to get angry. Human anger does not produce the righteousness God desires. (James 1:19-20 - NLT).

- A gentle answer deflects anger, but harsh words make tempers flare. (Proverbs 15:1 - NLT).

- A hot-tempered person starts fights; a cool-tempered person stops them. (Proverbs 15:18 - NLT).

- Don't befriend angry people or associate with hot-tempered people. (Proverbs 22:24 - NLT).

- Get rid of all bitterness, rage, anger, harsh words, and slander, as well as all types of evil behaviour. (Ephesians 4:31 – NLT).

- But I say, if you are even angry with someone, you are subject to judgment! If you call someone an idiot, you are in danger of being brought before the court. And if you curse someone, you are in danger of the fires of hell. (Matthew 5:22 - NLT).

- An angry person starts fights; a hot-tempered person commits all kinds of sin. (Proverbs 29:22 - NLT).

- A person without self-control is like a city with broken-down walls. (Proverbs 25:28 - NLT).

- In every place of worship, I want men to pray with holy hands lifted up to God, free from anger and controversy. (1 Timothy 2:8 - NLT).
- Hot-tempered people must pay the penalty. If you rescue them once, you will have to do it again. (Proverbs 19:19 - NLT).
- Better to be patient than powerful; better to have self-control than to conquer a city. (Proverbs 16:32 - NLT).

What Triggers Anger

- Threatened or attacked
- Frustrated or powerless
- Unfair treatment
- Disrespecting our feelings or possessions
- Fears
- Unmet needs or expectations
- Rejection
- Stress
- Financial challenges
- Unhealthy working environment

Effects of Anger

1. Physical effects – this includes increased anxiety, high blood pressure, and headaches.
2. Damaged interpersonal relationships.
3. Affects your self-esteem negatively.

4. Cause dysfunctionalities in children.
5. Strained relationships at work

The Root Cause of Anger

- Unresolved issues and unhealed hurts.
- Unmet needs – when there are unmet needs, then it is typical for frustration to develop.
- Failings and failures – this is especially devasting if it is a never-ending cycle from which it appears difficult to break free from.
- Disappointments in life – these could include relationship breakup, not being successful despite age, and the uncertainties that come with that.
- Curses – whether generational or personal (see Genesis 49:5-7).
- Envy/Jealousy – Saul, over the exploits of David, wanted to kill him.
- Rejection – not feeling a sense of acceptance and belonging. Struggling with approval addiction, for example, David and his family and Goliath.
- Missed opportunities – due to lack of focus, irresponsible behaviour, unqualified, not good enough, unprepared, or underprepared.

Results of Anger

- Lack of trust.
- Emotional upheaval and instability.

- Abuse of others (emotional, physical, and psychological).
- Self-destructive tendencies – Saul became suicidal.
- Mental breakdown.
- Bitterness – unfair treatment and resentment.
- Violence – developing evil intentions to the point of wishing to commit and even committing murder.
- Cruelty to others and self.
- Spiritual drought (no growth).
- Prayers being hindered.
- Lack of generosity.
- Confusion – cannot understand why the person that hurt you is prospering, and there is no evidence of remorse.
- Leads to rage and retaliation (will undermine and influence others against you).
- Condemns rather than elevate others.
- Self-pity – feels like everyone is against you.
- Highly critical of self and others.
- Unreasonable expectations.
- Use anger as a means of controlling others.
- Speaking in a condescending manner to others.

How to be Released from Anger

- Identify that you are angry.
- Identify why you are angry.
- Admit to the truth.
- Be willing to change (this requires humility).

- Deal with pride (stop covering up).
- Forgive others, self, and God.
- Confession of sins.
- Trust Jesus for cleansing and strength.
- Be a part of an accountability group.
- Submit to counselling from a skilled helper.

Added Advice

- Think before you speak.
- Use humour to release tension.
- Know when to seek help.
- Learn and practice how to relax.
- Apologise to those hurt by your actions.

Chapter 5

Unfailing Faith

Simon, Simon, Satan has asked to sift each of you like wheat. But I have pleaded in prayer for you, Simon, that your faith should not fail. So when you have repented and turned to me again, strengthen your brothers. (Luke 22:31-32 - NLT).

Faith is taking the first step, even when you don't see the whole staircase. – Martin Luther King Jr.

Many of us wrestle with the fear of failing. This represents a constant threat to our overall well-being. This constant fear can result in insecurities causing us to cave in under pressure.

One thing is evident is that failing does not make us failures, and rather than being devastated, we can learn from it and move forward.

With the ministry of Jesus on earth rapidly ending, there were several critical steps that He employed to prepare His disciples. He had indicated that after His departure, the Holy Spirit would come to make His abode in the lives of the believers. The Holy Spirit would play a critical role in guiding and providing spiritual strength to overcome.

Jesus' interaction with the disciples during the last supper is quite insightful and indeed informative. It shows us that God will always institute a survival plan for His people in the face of impending threats. Swirling around were many issues of which Jesus was aware, namely:

1. Hostility and the coming persecution storm.
2. Contention among the group regarding greatness.
3. Orchestrated attack by spiritual forces.

Jesus, up to this point, had borne the brunt of the enemy's attack. This factor was about to change, and the believers were going to be in harm's way. All believers have therefore become the object of the devil's wrath. No wonder Jesus emphasised that the disciples be on high alert lest they succumb to temptations. This advice is also relevant and pertinent to this time.

Keep watch and pray, so that you will not give in to temptation. For the spirit is willing, but the body is weak. (Matthew 26:41 - NLT).

The devil and his cohort's activities were not limited to that time only. We in this age need to be vigilant as we take on board the admonition of Peter.

Stay alert! Watch out for your great enemy, the devil. He prowls around like a roaring lion, looking for someone to devour. Stand firm against him, and be strong in your faith. Remember that your family of believers all over the world is going through the same kind of suffering you are. (1 Peter 5:8-9 - NLT).

Satan Has Asked for You

Through this narrative, we get an insight into the operations within the spiritual realm. We see our adversary actively involved in scheming and planning the demise of the believing community. In the case of Peter, he had asked for and received permission to attack. He therefore had the right to do so. We see both a demand and an insistence by the adversary.

We see a similar scenario in the Old Testament book of Job, where Satan was given permission to afflict Job.

Then the LORD asked Satan, "Have you noticed my servant Job? He is the finest man in all the earth. He is blameless— a man of complete integrity. He fears God and stays away from evil." Satan replied to the LORD, "Yes, but Job has good reason to fear God. You have always put a wall of protection around him and his home and his property. You have made him prosper in everything he does. Look how rich he is! But reach out and take away everything he has, and he will surely curse you to your face!" "All right, you may test him," the LORD said to Satan. "Do whatever you want with everything he possesses, but don't harm him

59

physically." So Satan left the LORD's presence. *(Job 1:8-12 - NLT).*

Peter, unlike Job, was not perfect, but his potential had caught the attention of the adversary. We need to bear in mind that our imperfections will not stop the devil from attacking us. He is not after our past; he is after our future. It is evident from the scriptures that bad things can happen to good people. We may be singled out as a test of our character (spiritual formation).

Purpose of the Enemy

The enemy's agenda was clear-cut. This extended not just to Peter but to all the disciples present, and I would dare say to us today that they would be sifted as wheat. The sifting process results in the shaking of the wheat in a sieve to separate the grain from the trash. All other extraneous materials picked up are separated in the process and removed, allowing only that which is vital to pass through.

Sifting will cause friction, upheavals, uncertainty, being pulled away and pulled apart. It will create instability and cause questioning of the circumstances of life. Jesus made it clear that all would be under pressure, and none would be exempt. The same conditions remain today. The enemy is unrelenting in his quest to create instability in our lives and to weaken our trust and resolve in God.

Peter's bold claims of readiness reveal his courage, but this courage was more so in his own strength than in that which God provides. Let us be aware that we stand or fall based on our dependence and reliance upon God. The admonition still holds true that we must not be fearful but cautious. We can only be victorious in our tests and temptations in the strength that the Lord provides.

If you think you are standing strong, be careful not to fall. (1 Corinthians 10:12 - NLT).

Jesus' Declaration

Jesus supplied the reassurance that all would need to hear, "I have prayed for you." This prayer provided the unconditional guarantee that the matter in terms of the outcome was already settled or pre-determined. Jesus was not promising a removal from the situation, but protection in it was inferred. This is further corroborated by Jesus' prayer in John 17:

I have given them your word. And the world hates them because they do not belong to the world, just as I do not belong to the world. I'm not asking you to take them out of the world, but to keep them safe from the evil one. They do not belong to this world any more than I do. (John 17:14-16 - NLT).

Unfailing Faith

Jesus' prayer will not go unanswered. This prayer reveals what God's intentions clearly are. We will not give up or quit like Peter despite the pressures. This prayer was going to insulate the disciples and present an effective barrier against the enemies' onslaughts. His faith would not be extinguished, and neither would he become spiritually bankrupt.

Promise and Prophecy

Jesus's remark reflected both a promise and a prophecy—*when you have returned (converted, turned back)*. Peter was going to recover from the shock to his faith and from the crisis that developed. He would gain strength over his weakness and be fully restored, returning to a state of spiritual viability. It is important that, like Peter, we learn from our experiences. The entire group was scattered, and the individuals suffered personally. Peter was tasked with the mandate of strengthening the brethren on his return.

Things to Consider

1. Stop being unrealistic about your own readiness to deal with the challenges of life.
2. None of us are immune to shaking, testing and tribulations.
3. Prayer is the key that allows us to bear up under pressure.

4. Jesus' intercessory role will shield us from being destroyed by the enemy.

5. Tests and challenges have a tendency to mature us in our faith.

Chapter 6

Faith Under Fire

Where There is Faith There is Fire)

Nebuchadnezzar said to them, "Is it true, Shadrach, Meshach, and Abednego, that you refuse to serve my gods or to worship the gold statue I have set up? I will give you one more chance to bow down and worship the statue I have made when you hear the sound of the musical instruments. But if you refuse, you will be thrown immediately into the blazing furnace. And then what god will be able to rescue you from my power?" (Daniel 3:14-15 - NLT).

*"The true measure of a man is not how he behaves in moments of comfort and convenience but **how he stands at times of controversy and challenges**." — Martin Luther King Jr.*

The Challenge of Acculturation

Babylon was governed by both a system and a philosophy of life. The main aim of Nebuchadnezzar in bringing these captive young men to Babylon was to systematically acculturate them. Acculturation deals with the assimilation into a different culture, which is normally the dominant or prevailing one. The process of acculturation will result in assimilation and integration into the dominant culture, which in this case would be Babylon.

A part of the acculturation process was to give them Babylonian names as opposed to retaining their Hebrew names. It is important to note that their identity and character were not affected by the name change.

The King achieved this through the process of educating young and impressionable minds. They were both mentored and schooled by a man whose sexuality had been tampered with (eunuch). His Job description was to teach them the language and culture of the Chaldeans. The period of instruction was to last for two years and at the end there would be an evaluation, then subsequent placement within society.

In a sense, the Hebrew young men were not victims but instruments in the hands of an omnipotent God (divine placement). God allowed them to be in Babylon so they would influence and affect the culture. Rather than being influenced, they were destined to be influencers. They were geographically distanced but still spiritually connected. Their faith in God was not based on location but on conviction. Despite them being young, they had an established Godly conviction and demonstrated unswerving loyalty to Him.

Ten Times Better

Civil disobedience is applicable, especially when it relates to matters of faith. Skillful negotiation undergirded by prayerful entreaty as opposed to heated confrontation was employed by Daniel in speaking with the prince of the eunuchs. Significant problems can sometimes be solved through respectful interaction. Being right should not mean being arrogant or disagreeable.

To the instruction that they partake of the meat and drink from the king's table that would oppose their dietary laws, a counter-proposal was advanced by Daniel. He requested permission for them to eat vegetables and drink water, then do an evaluation after ten days. This was not a fast but rather strict adherence to their dietary regime and practice. They were fully aware of the polytheistic and idolatrous culture that constituted Babylon, and knew that food from the king's table would have been dedicated to idols. It was a weighted decision not to conform to the norms.

At the end of the ten days, Daniel and his friends looked healthier and better nourished than the young men who had been eating the assigned food from the king's table. In addition, the four young men were given unusual aptitude and understanding from God in every aspect of literature and wisdom. Let us remember that excellence is not on break. God will always reward the efforts of the diligent. Daniel was given the special ability to interpret the meanings of visions and dreams.

At the end of the training period, upon examination, the king found them ten times more capable than the magicians and enchanters of the kingdom in all matters that required wisdom and balanced judgment. They were all given positions of authority within Babylon despite their faith. We must ensure that we not only thrive spiritually but in all aspects of our endeavours. This will bring much glory to God as our faith bears relevance in our everyday life.

Their Obedience to God Brought Special Favour

Believers currently can challenge societal norms and values that contradict the Word of God by their faith-based habits and diligent service. It is our faith that must inform our profession and practice. We can serve God as we are of service to society, even holding key and influential positions. It is not your societal position that informs your faith but rather your faith and conviction that influences your behaviour and conduct.

Climbing the ladder of social mobility could come about because of divine placement and must never be ignored. God will strategically position us where we can bring godly influence to bear as we operate based on convictions. It is important to marry faith with profession and avoid the dichotomy between faith and practice. For example, we are not Christians who happen to be Accountants, but rather we are Christian Accountants. Your faith must come first.

These men operated in civil offices, and it was not their preaching that influenced the society but rather their lives. Conduct and behaviour will speak more eloquently than words. To operate within our societies, we must begin to recognise, like the Hebrew men, that invaluable contributions can be made towards societal development in the world of work using spiritual principles. Not everything that is secular is evil. We must avoid or not be influenced by the profane as we seek to maintain consistency in our spirituality.

They Did Not Bow (Conform)

What many people call toleration is nothing more than compromise. There can be respect for a person's ability to make choices but not an acceptance of the choices they make that contravene biblical standards. The more society changes, the less accommodative it will become to faith-based people whose convictions are rooted in the God of the Bible. Faith that is tested can be trusted.

The command to worship the image that Nebuchadnezzar had set up in the plains of Dura was issued to all in Babylon, irrespective of their rank, religious persuasion, or social position (see Daniel 3). The worship of the image was meant to be a supreme test of allegiance to him. He was using religion to strengthen his grip on political power, much like what is done in our times. In this instance, there could be no separation of spiritual and national allegiance but a blend of both was being demanded.

Their reverence for God was far greater than their fear of men. They fully understood that there would be consequences to their acts of civil disobedience. Sometimes in serving God we must deviate from societal norms and expectations in favour of God and His holy standards. It is possible that the majority is not always right. We cannot allow peer pressure to cause us to go against the grain of our convictions. Godly decision-making may not be popular and can result in discrimination, severe punishment, and isolation.

The king's command was clear: at the sound of the music, fall down and worship the image or be cast immediately into the midst of a burning fiery furnace. The command was backed up by a threat, which demonstrated that the refusal to worship the image was not just a religious offense but tantamount to treason. The role of music in all forms of worship cannot be ignored. Music can both influence and inspire behaviour practices for good or evil. Music is not just lyrics and sound but a message that is being communicated to influence behaviour and conduct. It was all about worship and allegiance.

The threat, rather than causing fear, reposed confidence in God. Most of the crowd, as they were hearing the music, were falling in worship, but the three Hebrew men stood their ground. Non-conformity led to them being singled out and accused. Their failure to worship was met with strong disapproval by other officials who whether by political motivations or jealousy reported them. The Hebrew men did not lodge a formal complaint or protest but rather refrained from sharing in the sin of idolatry.

They preferred to obey God rather than man, even though they knew their stand would not go undetected. They did not hide or compromise but were willing to face the consequences of their actions.

They Did Not Bend

On hearing the report, the king summoned them to see whether they would deny or defend the accusation. He wanted to rely on the evidence rather than hearsay. They were now presented with a unique opportunity to compromise and evade the punishment. Serving God carries a premium cost. Consistency in service is demanded rather than a one-time show of adherence. We need to know and appreciate that it is not about the crowd, it is about our convictions. The pressure associated with their stand was enormous, but they refused to relent. The renewed charge by the king was bend (change) or burn. With impunity and disdain, the king declared that no god could deliver them from the punishment. He saw himself as the supreme being in Babylon, and so insulted all other gods. We need to stand fast even when the tide changes and we find ourselves hostages in a hostile situation.

The position of the Hebrew men was that "We don't need to defend ourselves. We are guilty of not conforming to your system of worship." They had a good appreciation and understanding of God's power. They were confident in God's omnipotence but also knew they were submitted to whatever would be His will in this situation. God could deliver, but if He did not, they were resolute and would not change their minds.

They did not equate the current challenges with an abandonment by God but rather understood that His will would be accomplished. They had great faith and extraordinary confidence that God would bless their obedience. They had obeyed God in the challenge of impure foods and so saw the test of fire as just another opportunity to prove God. There was a blunt refusal to follow the path of least resistance and so compromise. God was still God, whether in Judah or Babylon. Where we are located should never adversely influence what we believe about God. They placed a premium on obedience to God over and above all other facets of their lives. They were willing to lose everything for the sake of their Godly convictions. No excuses were convenient to justify any departure from their convictions.

They Did Not Burn

Oftentimes, our godly stand may anger those without our sense of convictions. The king was enraged, but the men were not intimidated. They had confessed their faith and would not relent. Not even the furnace being heated seven times hotter was enough to make them change their minds. They stood up as strong men in difficult times who had a solid relationship with God.

God did not allow the flames to devour them. Those who were charged with throwing them into the fire all died because of the flames. God miraculously intervened and they were spared. In fact, by the king's own admission, he was shocked that they survived in the furnace when others perished at the door. Not only were they alive, but they were loosed unharmed and walking around. God used this to divinely reveal Himself to the king, who now attested to the greatness of the God of the Hebrews.

We would do well to consider the admonition of Apostle Peter concerning times of adversity. We must not be surprised or alarmed but rejoice that we are sharing in the sufferings of Christ.

Dear friends, don't be surprised at the fiery trials you are going through, as if something strange were happening to you. Instead, be very glad—for these trials make you partners with Christ in his suffering, so that you will have the wonderful joy of seeing his glory when it is revealed to all the world. (1 Peter 4:12-13 - NLT).

Chapter 7

It Is Enough

Elijah was afraid and fled for his life. He went to Beersheba, a town in Judah, and he left his servant there. Then he went on alone into the wilderness, traveling all day. He sat down under a solitary broom tree and prayed that he might die. "I have had enough, LORD," he said. "Take my life, for I am no better than my ancestors who have already died." (1 Kings 19:3-4 - NLT).

Discouragement is not the absence of adequacy but the absence of courage. — Neal A. Maxwell

---

If there is a single character in the Bible who appeals to us based on his exemplary life of faith and faithfulness to God, it would be Elijah. He is well known, not only for his devotion to God, but for the extraordinary miraculous acts that accompanied his life of service to God and the people.

Elijah was as human as we are, and yet when he prayed earnestly that no rain would fall, none fell for three and a half years! Then, when he prayed again, the sky sent down

*rain and the earth began to yield its crops. (James 5:17-18
- NLT).*

Elijah the Tishbite's ministry was primarily to the Northern
Kingdom of Israel which was governed by the weak King
Ahab and his manipulative, idolatrous wife, Jezebel, who
promoted the worship of the pagan god, Baal. It was said of
Ahab that he did more wickedly than all the other kings
before him, which resulted in the judgment of God on the
nation.

Elijah's ministry was to this apostate nation to heed the call
of God to return. The withholding of rain and the subsequent
famine were the means selected to get the attention of the
people. In this act, God extended a sweeping challenge to
the fertility gods embraced by the people to which they had
no answer. Three and a half years was the time allocated for
the judgment.

He Knew God's Presence

Elijah's passionate communication with God characterised
the life of the man. He lived in the presence of the Almighty
and was devoted to a lifestyle of prayer. Elijah was relevant
and had a message as the spokesman of God to the nation.
The message resulted in drought, famine, social and
economic upheavals, and the persecution of the messenger.
During this time of austerity, Elijah experienced God's
providential care, protection, and provision supernaturally.

He Knew God's Power

At the end of the stated three and half years, Elijah requested to see Ahab, who saw him as the reason for the nation's distress.

When Ahab saw him, he exclaimed, "So, is it really you, you troublemaker of Israel?" (1 Kings 18:17 - NLT).

The reason for the nation's dilemma, Elijah stated, was attributed to their forsaking the commandments of God and the worshipping of pagan deities. Elijah's request was clear: let altars be prepared and each side offer prayer to their God to respond by fire. This was now brought into the arena of the battle of the gods. This power-encounter would once and for all prove who was truly the God of the nation, Israel.

The prayer of Elijah, unlike his antagonists, resulted in a sudden and dramatic manifestation and demonstration of power upon which the people acknowledged who the true God was, and the drought was broken.

Struggling With the Pressure of the Assignment

It is important to recognise that the most significant battle Elijah had to win was not external but more so internal. We must truly consider the mental strain that this man of God was labouring under based on the role he played as God's standard-bearer to the nation.

Despite what appeared to be insurmountable odds, his faith in God seemed up to the test. The first hint of a problem was in believing that he was alone in ministry.

Then Elijah said to them, "I am the only prophet of the Lord who is left, but Baal has 450 prophets." (1 Kings 18:22 - NLT).

Involvement in spiritual exercises can take a toll physically, mentally, and emotionally. The wear and tear of constant engagement without perceived support from the believing community can leave one exposed and vulnerable. Extreme exhaustion and loneliness can lead to despair and challenge even the most committed. Spiritual insights and victories should never make you less dependent on God but rather more trusting and open.

The Mount Carmel experience represented a major triumph of good over evil and true worship against paganism with their pantheon of gods. We must never lose sight of the condition of the man, despite what appears to be his spiritual prowess. Elijah, we are made aware through the scriptures, was as human as we are (see James 5:17). Spiritual advancement and victories do not make us less human or beyond the ability to be pressured by challenges. The true mettle of how we fare is the ability to which we bring balance and order into our lives as we continue to trust and depend on God.

The Breaking Point

Spiritual triumphs can cause us to become careless, seeing ourselves as invincible. What we hear can either establish or weaken. Elijah stood up to Ahab and the false prophets but fell prey to Jezebel's threat. It is often that one straw that breaks the proverbial camel's back.

When Ahab got home, he told Jezebel everything Elijah had done, including the way he had killed all the prophets of Baal. So Jezebel sent this message to Elijah: "May the gods strike me and even kill me if by this time tomorrow I have not killed you just as you killed them." (1 Kings 19:1-2 - NLT).

The very soul of Elijah was pierced by her words, and he suddenly lost confidence. He felt inadequate and exposed. In the heat of the moment, his whole world caved in and he gave up. He was overwhelmed by a flood of emotions that only facilitated his own insecurities. He had won a battle, but he was in danger of losing the war. His overactive mind only intensified the pressures to find a means of escaping. He could no longer stand, so he quit and ran for his life. Sometimes what influences us from without is based on what we harbour within. The real threat to Elijah was not so much Jezebel but himself.

The threat only served to reveal the frailty of the man in dealing with the enormity of mental pressures. What can we say about Elijah:

- He was tired and weary from the constant spiritual battles.
- He had internalised too much, and it pushed him to the breaking point.
- His confidence was shaken.
- External threats caused internal pressures.
- He thought Carmel would be the end of all conflicts.
- He wanted isolation.
- He was both lonely and alone.
- His energy was sapped.
- Insecurity led to fears and, subsequently, depression.
- Elijah was in meltdown mode.
- His trust and confidence were eroded.

The Prayer That God Did Not Answer

Then he went on alone into the wilderness, traveling all day. He sat down under a solitary broom tree and prayed that he might die. "I have had enough, LORD," he said. "Take my life, for I am no better than my ancestors who have already died." (1 Kings 19:4 - NLT).

Discouragement did not stop Elijah from praying. His prayer was borne out of anguish and frustration. His pitiful prayer spoke largely about the problems but reposed no confidence in God.

His unstable mental condition gave way to suicidal thoughts. He had given up the fight, and his death wish was that God would kill him and not Jezebel. He had lost all sense of meaning to his life and had abandoned purposeful living. Elijah was overwhelmed and lacked the stamina to continue. His strength was now depleted, and he had accepted both failure and defeat. He had finally succumbed and surrendered to the mental weight he was carrying for so long.

He was crushed by his own disappointments in himself that he became overwhelmed. "No more," he cried, "it is enough." This was not a resolution to go further but a resignation that it was over. He could not bother and did not want to be bothered. He blamed his failure on his own unworthiness. He considered himself then as much a sinner as his ancestors and so not deserving of life. Sometimes on route to depression, we make unfair comparisons and uniformed judgments. This idea of self-abasement was ill-conceived, informed by his own sense of having failed in his mission to return godliness to Israel. It is important to note that he was nourished physically then spiritually. We must never refrain from one at the expense of the other. The spirit and the body are both in need of nutrition.

The thoughts you entertain can either oppress or liberate you. What you occupy your mind with will ultimately influence the quality of your decision-making. Thoughts have a way of influencing behaviour. The greatest battles you will ever face in life are the internal ones that involve your thought life. The thoughts you entertain can either become a stronghold or a solution for breakthrough, healing, and deliverance.

The fight or flight response is typical when one feels under threat. Elijah had to learn you can run away from people, but you cannot outrun your thoughts. He had become incarcerated in a mental prison from which he saw no available means of escape. He chose to die rather than live in this level of bondage, but when we give up on ourselves and life, God has not given up on us.

God was noticeably and uncomfortably silent during this initial prayer request. He allowed Elijah to sleep and be ministered to before He spoke. God demonstrated that He is concerned with both our physical and spiritual needs. Sometimes the most spiritual thing you can do is to rest and recover for the next phase of the assignment. We must never underestimate the value of rest to recharge and reset our lives. Even Jesus would encourage His disciples to withdraw from ministry to rest. Rest offers the opportunity to recuperate and be refreshed and revitalised. This will allow for renewal with respect to our relationship with God. Withdrawal from the frontline can come through a crisis experience or through understanding when respite is in order. It is during those moments of withdrawal that the scars picked up in the heat of conflict can be healed and our souls restored.

The apostles returned to Jesus from their ministry tour and told him all they had done and taught. Then Jesus said, "Let's go off by ourselves to a quiet place and rest awhile." He said this because there were so many people coming and going that Jesus and his apostles didn't even have time to eat. So they left by boat for a quiet place, where they could be alone. (Mark 6:30-32 - NLT).

Recovery from the breaking point will require being open to ministry. Those who are always serving themselves will need to be served. Those who are ministering will also need ministry. God is committed to not only providing the conviction to serve but also the season of refreshing. Taking a break is critical to your mental health. In the old covenant, God told Israel to labour for six days but rest on the seventh. Never allow the rigors of ministry to disrupt your life to the point where there is no balance between rest and work. Taking care of your body through rest, exercise, and proper nutrition is critical to your overall spiritual well-being.

From the ends of the earth, I cry to you for help when my heart is overwhelmed. Lead me to the towering rock of safety. (Psalm 61:2 - NLT).

There is nothing like recognising our needs but knowing where we can draw strength from. There is indeed a place in God where recovery will take place. Sometimes God will be waiting patiently until we come to the end of our own sufficiency and recognise that He is all-sufficient.

God set Elijah on a 200-mile, 40-day trip to Mount Horeb, also known as Mount Sinai. This shows that God did not demand an immediate recovery from Elijah. He allowed the prophet time to recover from his spiritual depression. The trip could have been shorter, taking a quarter of that time, but Elijah needed time to recover from his spiritual defeatist attitude. It is important that we take the time needed and avoid shortcuts.

Finding God in Retreating

Elijah, in running away from the vicissitudes of life, came face to face with the comfort and consolation of the eternal God. He retreated to a cave and spent a night in the dark. It was in his retreating that he had a larger-than-life encounter with God.

Rather than rebuke, God used a question to probe Elijah's plight. It was not a means of giving him a reason to justify his current situation but rather to evaluate. Since God oversaw Elijah's life only, he could conclude the duration of his ministry. This question was reminiscent of what God asked Adam in the garden (see Genesis 3:9). It was clear that Elijah was out of position. Elijah was about to see God as an encourager amid his discouragement. It was not a rebuke that Elijah needed but reassurance. The question God asked allowed Elijah an opportunity to vent. God is not trying to shut us up; He is facilitating our communication with Him. It was in speaking freely that he would unburden his heart from its previous complications.

Elijah's Perception on What Transpired

- Faithful service but life in danger.
- The unfairness of his current distress.

- The killing of God's prophets.
- Feelings of isolation ("I alone am left").
- Spoke to his own fears.
- The deplorable spiritual state of the nation.
- The rise in idolatry and the repression of true worship.

There is nothing like a fresh experience with God to give us a new perspective and revive us. God gave Elijah a personal encounter that stabilised the relationship. God is not always in the dramatic; He can be heard in the stillness and quiet of our hearts. Elijah had seen the powerful display of God's power on Mount Carmel, but now he became sensitive to the personal care and attention on an individual plane. God speaks powerfully in the silence of our hearts as we quiet ourselves before Him.

God reassured Elijah concerning the facts. "You are not alone, and there are 7000 that have not compromised but remained committed." Sometimes it is not the miracles but our daily living that becomes the hallmark of encouragement for others. Integrity is a greater example than demonstrations of power. Sometimes discouragement and disillusionment come because we are not seeing things from God's perspective. Elijah thought that his vindication on Mount Carmel would have changed the spiritual condition of the nation, but unknown to him, there was an army of individuals whose faith had become stronger because of his stance. They adamantly refused to give in to the threat of paganism and remained wholly dedicated to the service of God.

Once Elijah was refreshed, God gave him a fresh perspective on both his life and continuance in ministry. Elijah was to anoint Ahab's successor in the person of Jehu. He was given a trusted friend and devoted companion in the person of his successor, Elisha, and Hazael was anointed as king over Syria. All these became sources of encouragement to Elijah that boosted his confidence and unswerving loyalty to God.

With these God-given promises, he knew that, ultimately, justice would be done, and God would not allow the institutionalized persecution and promotion of idolatry to go unpunished.

Chapter 8

Renewed Mind for a Transformed Life

And so, dear brothers and sisters, I plead with you to give your bodies to God because of all he has done for you. Let them be a living and holy sacrifice—the kind he will find acceptable. This is truly the way to worship him. Don't copy the behavior and customs of this world, but let God transform you into a new person by changing the way you think. Then you will learn to know God's will for you, which is good and pleasing and perfect. (Romans 12:1-2 - NLT).

I will not let anyone walk through my mind with their dirty feet. – Mahatma Gandhi

The mind is commonly referred to as the principal battleground. This is where the most intense of spiritual battles occur. The mind is the very seat of consciousness, and this is where you have the intellect, emotion, and will. Our thought life determines our vulnerability or stability. The mind was affected by the fall of man. Our thoughts influence our course of action.

Thoughts are responsible for our mental and emotional well-being.

The mind is that part of the soul that is responsible for thought and influences actions. It is the seat of understanding and conscious ability. There needs to be a transference of allegiance where unhealthy patterns of thinking must go.

Conformed

To be molded or stamped according to a pattern, there is the need to actively resist what is attempting to squeeze us into its shape. The world's systems and philosophies will create undue pressures. Ensure that you do not become so well adjusted to the ungodly culture that you fit in without even thinking. We must avoid being fashioned by this age.

1. Do not adopt or adapt to the lifestyle and practices of the world.
2. Do not imitate or pattern the fashion and lusts of this world.

Do not love this world nor the things it offers you, for when you love the world, you do not have the love of the Father in you. For the world offers only a craving for physical pleasure, a craving for everything we see, and pride in our achievements and possessions. These are not from the Father, but are from this world. (1 John 2:15-16 - NLT).

3. Do not follow the course of this world.

You used to live in sin, just like the rest of the world, obeying the devil—the commander of the powers in the unseen world. He is the spirit at work in the hearts of those who refuse to obey God. (Ephesians 2:2 - NLT).

4. Do not follow the god of this age (world). (see 2 Corinthians 4:4).
5. Do not follow the leaders of this world. (see 1 Corinthians 2:6-8).
6. Do not follow the deceitfulness of riches of this world and be consumed by the acquisition of things and not God. If unbridled, this will eventually choke one's spiritual life.
7. Do not live in carnal pleasure.
8. Do not follow the crowd in evil. You need to war against the tide of sin, self, and Satan.

Issues of tolerance/compromise bombard the world's philosophy. The current tide or trend is a belief in no moral absolutes. It is no longer black or white, good or evil, or moral and immoral. Everything is now blurred with no clear lines of separation (shades of grey). The world is characterised by unnatural influences, which tend to lead you away from a vital relationship with God.

Christ has the power to enable us to live a transformed life. It is through our repentance that change comes. The evidence is irrefutable that a renewal will only come through repentance and the experience of the new birth.

Transformation

The word for transformation is *Metamorphosis* which means an outward, permanent change. It is the changing from one form to another, for example, a tadpole to a frog or a caterpillar to a butterfly. These changes in transformation are deemed irreversible and permanent. In considering spiritual transformation, the following must be borne in mind:

1. It is a continuous process of change.
2. God is the catalyst of the change.
3. We have a personal responsibility to surrender to His influence and will.
4. The presentation of ourselves to God is our personal responsibility.
5. Being a living sacrifice is what God demands.
6. The presentation of ourselves is deemed our spiritual act of worship to God.

Transformation requires a radical shift. It is the breaking of an already established pattern that we have become accustomed to. This means that we resist and are unwilling to yield or surrender. Transformation can only take place through the renewing of the mind, that produces an inward change with outward manifestations. It is not possible to avoid worldly behaviours and conduct without first being transformed. Transformation is not simply a mental switch from the not-to-do list to the to-do list; it is the transforming power of the Holy Spirit within our lives that creates change and not adjustments. Transformation is not just about the acquisition of more knowledge but a surrendering to the Holy Spirit, who renews our minds and allows us to live a new spiritual life.

Change the Way You Think

Rules can never deliver us from bondage. Never use the mind to suppress the truth of God's Word. The cult of self tends to undermine the authority of Christ, seeking to establish its own righteousness separate and apart from God. It is possible to be a Christian and not enjoy the freedom of the Christ-life because of the bondage and slavery to sin.

We need to stop giving sin the right of way by constantly yielding to the pressure. It is possible to get tired of fighting and not winning and so give up and give in. As believers, we cannot establish faith on a dual citizenship; a choice will have to be made. We can love God but not reverence Him because of an addiction to the pleasures derived from sinful conduct.

Forgiveness in no way endorses indulgence. We must stop surrendering our bodies to the whims and appetites of the lower nature. The renewed mind will interpret life through the lens of God's Word and the guidance of the Holy Spirit. It is the Spirit's empowerment that causes us to live the Spirit-filled life where we obey from the heart and are not just following rules and regulations. It is a day-to-day decision that is based on right choices that reflect the very character of Christ. Defeat is inevitable if the mind is not renewed.

The renewing of the mind aligns our minds to the truth of God's Word where we recognise the lies and deception of the enemy and replace and reinforce them with God's Word.

We use God's mighty weapons, not worldly weapons, to knock down the strongholds of human reasoning and to destroy false arguments. We destroy every proud obstacle that keeps people from knowing God. We capture their rebellious thoughts and teach them to obey Christ. (2 Corinthians 10:4-5 - NLT).

The idea of taking a thought captive means to capture or conquer that thought as you identify it and compare it to God's Word. Whenever the thoughts do not agree with the Word, it is rejected so that it does not have any undue influence on our lives. These thoughts are then replaced with God's promises from His Word.

Since thoughts fuel belief and actions, then renewal allows for Godly living where the general focus is on pleasing and serving God. Our thoughts create the boundaries for our lives. So, living for God now becomes intentional. With new desires, we have a strong inclination to do right and reject wrong.

The problem with the mind is not just that we are finite, but we are fallen. This mindset is hostile to God and must be changed. The mind, if allowed, will wilfully suppress the truth of God, making us slaves to passions and desires that would lose their hold if we knew God as we ought.

So prepare your minds for action and exercise self-control. Put all your hope in the gracious salvation that will come to you when Jesus Christ is revealed to the world. So you must live as God's obedient children. Don't slip back into your old ways of living to satisfy your own desires. You didn't know any better then. (1 Peter 1:13-14 - NLT).

We who have a relationship with Christ Jesus can throw off the old sinful nature as we allow the Spirit's renewal to change our thoughts, attitudes, and actions. We are now liberated through this new nature to live as God would have us to in true righteousness and holiness.

Since you have heard about Jesus and have learned the truth that comes from him, throw off your old sinful nature and your former way of life, which is corrupted by lust and deception. Instead, let the Spirit renew your thoughts and attitudes. Put on your new nature, created to be like God— truly righteous and holy. (Ephesians 4:21-24 - NLT).

Mind renewal causes us not to walk or live in wilful ignorance because of the darkness in the heart. As we surrender from the heart, we become liberated from the bondage.

With the Lord's authority I say this: Live no longer as the Gentiles do, for they are hopelessly confused. Their minds are full of darkness; they wander far from the life God gives because they have closed their minds and hardened their hearts against him. They have no sense of shame. They live for lustful pleasure and eagerly practice every kind of impurity. (Ephesians 4:17-19 - NLT).

It can be overemphasised that the Spirit renews the mind. We therefore are wholly dependent on Him and His influence. He enables us as we comply with His instructions.

He saved us, not because of the righteous things we had done, but because of his mercy. He washed away our sins, giving us a new birth and new life through the Holy Spirit. (Titus 3:5 - NLT).

The transformation that comes through mind-renewal is progressive in nature and requires us to be focused and disciplined. The Spirit exposes the mind to Christ-exalting truths and deals with the rebellion and stubbornness of the heart. We therefore develop an unconditional love for the life-transforming Word, express ourselves in undiluted worship, and practice being in the presence of Christ and being influenced by His glorious perfections.

So all of us who have had that veil removed can see and reflect the glory of the Lord. And the Lord—who is the Spirit—makes us more and more like him as we are changed into his glorious image. (2 Corinthians 3:18 - NLT).

The light of the glorious gospel of Christ has both a liberating and revelatory effect. We see ourselves; we see Christ, and we pursue that desire to be like Him in word and conduct. Remember, it must be a mind-change for life-change. We must find and follow God's will for our lives.

Mind Renewal Checklist

- Believe that it is Christ in you that causes the renewal by the Holy Spirit as we surrender to Him.
- God will finish the work He started in you.
- We must keep our minds on spiritual rather than carnal things.
- We must never allow the mind to be corrupted through deception.
- Saturate your mind with the Word (read and study).
- Commit the Word to memory and take heed to it.
- Break decisively every unholy and unwholesome thought and communication.
- Do not fulfil the desires of the flesh and mind.
- Ask for and possess the mind of Christ.
- Obey God from the heart.
- Establish and maintain boundaries.
- Be sensitive to God's will and be committed to submit and obey.
- Reinforce in your thinking that it is an empowerment that is needed and not a new set of rules to deal with the breaking of the old ones.
- Set your mind on things above (maintain your focus).

Let us all endorse and apply the words of Paul to the Philippians in our quest for mind renewal:

And now, dear brothers and sisters, one final thing. Fix your thoughts on what is true, and honorable, and right, and pure, and lovely, and admirable. Think about things that are excellent and worthy of praise. Keep putting into practice all you learned and received from me—everything you heard from me and saw me doing. Then the God of peace will be with you. (Philippians 4:8-9 - NLT).

Chapter 9

Tried By the Word

They bruised his feet with fetters and placed his neck in an iron collar. Until the time came to fulfill his dreams, the LORD tested Joseph's character. (Psalm 105:18-19 - NLT).

Life's trials are not easy. But in God's will, each has a purpose. – Warren Wiersbe

---

The revelation of God concerning your life will show you the destination but not necessarily the distance. Not every word will be fulfilled in an instant. The word will contain both a promise and a prophecy, but it will require you being processed. Knowing the future will never negate tests and trials that will be faced. The presence of problems is never the absence of God. There are problems faced that are primarily because of our relationship with God and others based on the purpose to be fulfilled. God will not reveal where He is not committed to leading. All the twists and turns in life have been considered and will not be able to stop the fulfilment of your destiny.

God will use adversity and adversaries to bring to fruition His Word concerning your future. He will never abdicate His responsibilities concerning you. God will finish what He started. There is the need to trust God as your only viable option and so patiently endure until the promise is fulfilled. The promise will highlight God's unfailing guarantee toward you. He is faithful that promised, and able to perform His will.

Sometimes the very people you are called to help will be the very ones who oppose you vehemently. Not everyone will embrace the idea that you are called to play a significant role in their lives. It is amazing how their distrust, abuse, rejection, and plots will serve the purpose intended by God.

Being called and chosen by God to accomplish His purpose on earth is often fraught with challenges. Being tested is not automatically a sign that we have lost our way or taken a spiritual detour. God has taken all things into consideration, and despite the twists and turns within the journey, the destination remains the same.

There were five distinct phases of life that Joseph went through before he articulated the conclusion that even adversity within his life still ended up serving God's purpose.

You intended to harm me, but God intended it all for good. He brought me to this position so I could save the lives of many people. (Genesis 50:20 - NLT).

His People

The strong correlation between adversity and God's purpose for us is clearly reflected in the life of Joseph. It demonstrates that being called of God for a particular purpose will never make us exempt from tests and challenges. How we navigate these will be a testimony to our faith, conviction, and overall submission to God's guidance.

What can be very alarming and unsettling is the intensity of challenges faced, especially from those close to us. This can be borne out of misunderstanding and jealousy or because they have taken offense based on our lives or conversations. Joseph would discover that between promise and purpose can come persecution and testing.

Extraordinary dreams have nothing to do with age, experience, birthing order, location, or family of origin. Not only was Joseph favoured by his father, which exposed the dysfunctionalities of his family, but he began to dream. The place of our dreams might not be the location of its fulfilment. Sibling hatred festered and grew because of the preferential treatment meted out to him by Jacob, his father, coupled with the perceived interpretation of his dreams by them.

What makes us stand out to others may become a source of irritation, conflict, and bother. The dreams Joseph related stirred up envy, strife, jealousy, and bitterness. Not everyone will cheer or be supportive of our potential successes. Our

99

dreams may intimidate or cause others to become resentful. The fact that Joseph dared to articulate the dream and the impact it would have on the family earned him a stern rebuke from his father and sustained hatred from his brothers. Joseph's prophetic dreams served to alienate his brothers from him. His dreams not only insulted his older brothers but were a clear violation of their customs and traditions. God's will for our lives may not conform to societal norms and expectations. Our dreams should challenge us but never make us fearful irrespective of how we are treated by others.

It is possible for scepticism to be rife because of familiarity and the fact that we dare to dream beyond the expectations of the community of which we are a part. God's will for our lives is never subject to human approval and endorsement. The dreams that God gave to Joseph did not require human consensus.

The Pit

God will allow controversy to facilitate a change of location in keeping with the journey that must be taken. God's way of doing things might contradict with our expectations. The outcome is guaranteed, even though the journey may be filled with tests. Sometimes in life things will get worse before it gets better.

The brothers initially conspired to kill him because they were fearful that his dreams would come through. They spoke contemptuously concerning him as a dreamer of dreams. They felt that if he were killed, his dreams would be aborted. God appearing to be silent does not mean He is not actively at work. Joseph being thrown into a pit might make his dreams appear to be delusions of grandeur. It was however an important aspect of the journey. What appears to be a disappointment to us may very well be God's will for our lives.

He was stripped of his coat, a symbol of preferential treatment by his father, Jacob, and cast into a dry pit by his brothers. The exposure did not diminish his worth or value to the plan of God. Despite the harshness of the treatment, he was right where God wanted him to be. The difficulty sometimes is being able to see things from God's perspective. This was not the end but rather a new beginning, albeit fraught with challenges. Sometimes hurting is helping.

Selling Joseph into slavery might appear to be demeaning and catastrophic from the perspective of the onlookers; however, it brought him one step closer to the nation that his giftings were going to have a considerable impact upon. Sometimes a devious and deceptive plot is literally playing into the hands of God; evil intentions fulfilling divine purpose.

Potiphar's House

What would characterise this phase of Joseph's life was the often-repeated phrase "and the Lord was with Joseph." Our attitude during testing times is critical to our spiritual and temporal mobility. During seasons of hardship, there must be both discipline and diligence to achieve the stated intent of the original dream. Our trust in God will cause us to endure untold hardships, knowing that He is still in charge of our lives. Being a good man and a man of God does not exempt us from adversity.

The LORD directs the steps of the godly. He delights in every detail of their lives. Though they stumble, they will never fall, for the LORD holds them by the hand. (Psalms 37:23-24 - NLT).

It is important that we maintain our communion and communication with God during the process to avail ourselves of the desired outcome. Not only was he successful but prosperous, even in a challenging environment. Despite his location changing, his faith in God remained steadfast.

Our serving others and devotion to God must be with excellence despite being in an unfavourable environment. Challenges must never make us bitter but better. On no occasion do we find Joseph being resentful or angry that, despite his sterling service to God, he was a slave in an Egyptian household. Joseph's advancements were due primarily to God's favour and his industry. With great authority comes great responsibility and accountability. His faith and convictions were not dependent on location. It is important to establish and maintain boundaries to avoid the corruption of ideals and moral standards. Not everything that appears to be good is godly.

Joseph was able to maintain integrity with respect to the management and handling of Potiphar's affairs. The integrity test came to a head with the attempted seduction by Potiphar's wife. His blunt refusal to be intimate with her despite the constant pressure incurred her wrath at being spurned. His refusal was based on his relationship with God and an unwillingness to betray the trust that Potiphar had placed in him. Her plan to force him when none of the men were in the house backfired as he ran outside leaving his garments in her hand. He ended up being punished for the stand taken and was sent to the prison where the king's prisoners were kept. Potiphar could have had Joseph killed, but his impeccable track record, coupled with God's favour, averted this disaster. God was not through with him yet. There are always consequences for Godly living. There are instances where one's reputation may be damaged in the eyes of people but intact in the sight of God. Doing the right thing may not end up in us being rewarded but criticised, punished, or even condemned.

When God is in control, our destiny is secure irrespective of the twists and turns taken in life. It is important that we keep the destination in mind while en route. Negative things happening does not mean there won't be a positive outcome. Everywhere Joseph went, God foreknew and would benefit the plan of God. Every single detail of his life was taken into consideration in revealing what his ultimate destiny would be.

The LORD directs the steps of the godly. He delights in every detail of their lives. Though they stumble, they will never fall, for the LORD holds them by the hand. (Psalm 37:23-24 - NLT).

The Prison

It is amazing that even with Joseph's prison experience, God was still with him. He received mercy and favour that allowed him to prosper even in confinement. Once we commit our ways to God, we can trust Him with regard to the outcome. Out of evil intentions, God can produce a wealth of good.

You can make many plans, but the LORD's purpose will prevail. (Proverbs 19:21 - NLT).

Excellence is not dependent on where we are but on who we are. We can make the best of a bad situation by consistently operating at a high standard and not feeding ourselves with negativity. We must have the resolve and determination coupled with an unbreakable spirit. Joseph knew this could not be the end because the dreams had not yet come through.

It was within the prison that the dreamer became the interpreter. His perspective on God and His plans never changed. We must never give up on ourselves and, certainly, never give up on God. His interpretation of the butler and
104

baker's dream was underscored by the statement that interpretations belong to God. Amid the challenges, Joseph maintained an active communion and communication with God. We must never allow adversities in life to cause us to doubt and become antagonistic to God. Joseph knew that the outcome was already predetermined: God was the driver and, he, a willing passenger on this journey. When we continue to walk faithfully with God, our destiny becomes unshakeable.

It is important that we rely more on God than man. Man's promises can be broken, but God's Word will forever stand. God will allow you to go into adversity, then, for His glory, bring you out.

And please remember me and do me a favor when things go well for you. Mention me to Pharaoh, so he might let me out of this place. For I was kidnapped from my homeland, the land of the Hebrews, and now I'm here in prison, but I did nothing to deserve it." Pharaoh's chief cup-bearer, however, forgot all about Joseph, never giving him another thought. (Genesis 40:14-15, 23 - NLT).

It is better to take refuge in the LORD than to trust in people. (Psalm 118:8 - NLT).

Joseph went through a series of pains and disappointments until the time came for the Word of God over his life to be fulfilled. God is strategic with respect to His interventions. It may not happen the way we think but how He intended. It took two years after the butler's release for God to cement His plan.

The Palace

Things can change dramatically when God is orchestrating the moves. Joseph's ascendency was to begin with Pharoah having a dream that no one could interpret. It was then that the butler remembered and gave a recommendation to Pharoah concerning Joseph and his ability to interpret dreams. We are here on this earth as problem-solvers, uniquely qualified and gifted, waiting on our time to be announced. Joseph interpreting Pharaoh's dreams brought his dreams to fruition.

When Joseph was brought from the prison to stand before Pharoah, pride or arrogance did not fill his heart. With humility, he indicated that God was his source, and He would respond.

"It is beyond my power to do this," Joseph replied. "But God can tell you what it means and set you at ease." (Genesis 41:16 - NLT).

Joseph revealed a national development plan that would ensure Egypt's and the surrounding nation's survival during the coming famine. We must trust God and wait on His timing for the release.

Then Pharaoh said to Joseph, "Since God has revealed the meaning of the dreams to you, clearly no one else is as
106

intelligent or wise as you are. You will be in charge of my court, and all my people will take orders from you. Only I, sitting on my throne, will have a rank higher than yours." Pharaoh said to Joseph, "I hereby put you in charge of the entire land of Egypt." (Genesis 41:39-41 - NLT).

Chapter 10

How To Handle Adversity

We are pressed on every side by troubles, but we are not crushed. We are perplexed, but not driven to despair. We are hunted down, but never abandoned by God. We get knocked down, but we are not destroyed. Through suffering, our bodies continue to share in the death of Jesus so that the life of Jesus may also be seen in our bodies. (2 Corinthians 4:8-10 – NLT).

Adversity is preparation for greatness. – Andy Andrews

The life of Apostle Paul is indeed a lesson in how submission to God allows us to deal with tests and temptations. Despite being graced with a tremendous ministry, he faced many obstacles and challenges. His response, despite the herculean pressures, was to repose trust and confidence in God. His conversion was a very dramatic one being struck down on the road to Damascus and hearing the voice of Jesus, which gave him a very clear-cut mandate concerning his life and ministry.

But the Lord said, "Go, for Saul is my chosen instrument to take my message to the Gentiles and to kings, as well as to the people of Israel. And I will show him how much he must suffer for my name's sake." (Acts 9:15-16 - NLT).

Paul indicated that suffering is a critical part of the Christian's life and witness. Paul is here acknowledging that faithfulness to God will lead to persecution from the ungodly world. This contrasts with the material wealth and prosperity being advocated by some. His life was reflective of what he taught, writing with so much joy and comfort from a prison cell as he awaited a pending death for his faith.

You know how much persecution and suffering I have endured. You know all about how I was persecuted in Antioch, Iconium, and Lystra—but the Lord rescued me from all of it. Yes, and everyone who wants to live a godly life in Christ Jesus will suffer persecution. (2 Timothy 3:11-12 - NLT).

Peter agreed with Paul that Christians should expect and be prepared to experience suffering in this life. The life of Christ showed that He endured enormous suffering, and His disciples should expect the same. We must not be surprised by the hardships of life and feel that God has betrayed or forsaken us. We must possess the same attitude that Christ did as we face these challenging times. Our walk with Christ, through suffering, will free us from the careless indulgence to sin through disobedience. We are not so caught up with the comforts and pleasures of this life that we fail to endure the discomforts and hardships associated

110

with our faith in Christ. There is the need to stay alert and be persistent in prayer as we endeavour to steer our lives away from sin, understanding the role that suffering play in fulfilling God's purpose in our lives.

So then, since Christ suffered physical pain, you must arm yourselves with the same attitude he had, and be ready to suffer, too. For if you have suffered physically for Christ, you have finished with sin. (1 Peter 4:1 - NLT).

Strength in Weakness

God can use suffering as a means of keeping us humble as we confidently depend upon His enabling ability to sustain us. Paul was conscious that he was not immune to the danger of pride based on his own spiritual experiences. He tells of the unique experience of the heavenly vision not to glorify himself but rather speak concerning his thorn in the flesh.

They saw Paul's thorn but knew nothing of his heavenly visions. People can think less of us because of the challenges we face, not knowing the reason we face them. Paul considered his challenges as a gift from God. The description of the term "thorn" signifies something akin to a stake rather than a splinter. This was not only frustrating but caused major troubles in the life of the afflicted.

Paul felt as if he was being beaten by the affliction permitted by God in allowing the messenger of Satan to buffet him. Sometimes being extremely blessed of God comes with

111

great pressures. Our appearance may belie the crisis being experienced. It is evident that the affliction made him feel weak and powerless. It was not a lack of faith or prayer partners that made the affliction continue.

Paul committed the situation in persistent (ceaseless) prayer to God, passionately entreating Him for deliverance. This problem affected him physically, mentally, and spiritually. The response was certainly not what Paul had anticipated. Instead of removing the thorn, God gave and would keep giving grace sufficient to keep him. God did not remove the load; He simply strengthened the shoulder.

This infirmity fostered total and complete dependency on God as his source of strength during moments of weakness. God became his source of strength. Paul was able to rejoice in the fact that God had used the adverse situation to cause complete reliance on Him through the adversity. The thorn provided an opportunity for a display of God's strength and power.

Even though I have received such wonderful revelations from God. So to keep me from becoming proud, I was given a thorn in my flesh, a messenger from Satan to torment me and keep me from becoming proud. Three different times I begged the Lord to take it away. Each time he said, "My grace is all you need. My power works best in weakness." So now I am glad to boast about my weaknesses, so that the power of Christ can work through me. That's why I take pleasure in my weaknesses, and in the insults, hardships, persecutions, and troubles that I suffer for Christ. For when I am weak, then I am strong. (2 Corinthians 12:7-10 - NLT).

Comfort In Suffering

Paul speaks to a relationship between suffering and God's power in his life and ministry. Some thought that he had suffered too much to be a spiritual apostle. Comfort in trials comes not just because of the hope of deliverance but because of God's continuous and abiding presence. We are certainly never left on our own.

God will certainly provide the strength to make us bravely face the tests and trials in our lives. Through God, Paul and, by extension, us will praise God despite the pain, knowing that God is committed to helping us patiently endure. Paul was testifying to his first-hand knowledge of the God of all comfort—the God who both strengthens and makes strong, not just providing soothing sympathy.

The greater purpose of the comfort that God provides is that we may reassure and comfort others. Our experience with God thus adds value to the lives of those within the spiritual community of believers. We should never allow pride to block us from receiving the ministry of others to us by not reaching out for help. We help as we encourage those going through the tests and temptations of life, that they too will be victorious.

Troubles in life never speak to the absence of God, but those experiences provide clarity and reward us with a testimony concerning the sufficiency of God. Suffering is not for the sake of competing to see who is more resilient under pressure. As suffering abounds, so does God's consolation. There is no need for anger and embarrassment during our struggles. In suffering, we are hurting but being assured by God. The consolation comes not just when the situation changes but the comfort that Christ provides during times of adversity.

All praise to God, the Father of our Lord Jesus Christ. God is our merciful Father and the source of all comfort. He comforts us in all our troubles so that we can comfort others. When they are troubled, we will be able to give them the same comfort God has given us. For the more we suffer for Christ, the more God will shower us with his comfort through Christ. (2 Corinthians 1:3-5 - NLT).

Rejoicing in Suffering

Our attitude in suffering runs contrary to popular expectations. Suffering would be the source of discouragement and hopelessness among many, but not so for the believer. We are to rejoice because we understand the benefits that will accrue. Paul acknowledges that what is being faced is not some minor inconvenience but real hardship. Yet he encourages all to glory in the discomfort because of what it produces in us. Suffering tends to aid in our spiritual formation as it builds endurance, patience, and character.

When we are tested, it puts the mettle of what we believe to extreme scrutiny. It enhances our spirituality through our dependency on God during those times. We do not despise God for allowing suffering into our lives, but we recognise that His love will cause us to be sustained during those times. We learn to love God despite the challenges.

We can rejoice, too, when we run into problems and trials, for we know that they help us develop endurance. And endurance develops strength of character, and character strengthens our confident hope of salvation. And this hope will not lead to disappointment. For we know how dearly God loves us, because he has given us the Holy Spirit to fill our hearts with his love. (Romans 5:3-5 - NLT).

Why We Rejoice in Suffering

- It is a slight momentary affliction that prepares for something far more significant (see 2 Corinthians 4:17).
- Suffering prepares us to reign and be glorified with Christ (see Romans 8:17).
- It is the opportunity we have to follow the example of Christ (see 2 Peter 2:21).
- It matures us in the faith and our relationship with Christ as we anticipate what is ahead (see 1 Peter 1:7).

115

- God is intentional in the challenges that we are allowed to face.
- We derive much wisdom and empathy from it.
- God will never leave us in times of hardship.

Dear friends, don't be surprised at the fiery trials you are going through, as if something strange were happening to you. Instead, be very glad—for these trials make you partners with Christ in his suffering, so that you will have the wonderful joy of seeing his glory when it is revealed to all the world. But it is no shame to suffer for being a Christian. Praise God for the privilege of being called by his name! (1 Peter 4:12-13, 16 - NLT).

Sharing in Christ's sufferings should bring about tremendous joy among the believing community. The fiery trials we endure now purify and must never be seen as punishment. Christians and the ungodly will suffer the same things; however, the purpose and effect are different. The believer's suffering is never a source of embarrassment but rather a call to be joyous.

Standing Strong

Paul's suffering was an encouragement to others to persevere through their adversities. He emphasises in 2 Corinthians 4:8-10 that he had afflictions without and fears within. He faced the conspiracy of some that had bound themselves to an oath not to eat or drink until they had murdered him (see Acts 23:12). Despite all that he faced, he was not crushed by the stress of it all. He still served the Lord gloriously with deep convictions.

Despite seeing no way out as he felt hunted by those endeavouring to destroy him, he knew God had not forsaken him and that through his experiences, he was being strengthened. God spared his life on numerous occasions so that he could continue sharing the good news.

There are some aspects of God's great work that will only happen through trials and suffering in our lives. Jesus' death was not just a historical fact but a spiritual reality in Paul's life. Our effectiveness as servants of God will be greatly enhanced through our sufferings and provide a credible witness to others.

Chapter 11

Restoring the Fallen

Dear brothers and sisters, if another believer is overcome by some sin, you who are godly should gently and humbly help that person back onto the right path. And be careful not to fall into the same temptation yourself. Share each other's burdens, and in this way obey the law of Christ. (Galatians 6:1-2 - NLT).

The work of restoration cannot begin until a problem is fully faced. – Dan B. Allender

---

Restoration has always been a major theme in scripture and truly reflects the very heart and nature of God. Those who have benefited from restoration should themselves be willing to play an important role in bringing the message of restoration. It is God's unfailing love that makes this possible. He is not trying to destroy but rather redeem humanity. Restoration is deemed necessary because of man's disobedience to God, which resulted in estrangement, broken fellowship, and communion.

Defining restoration:

- To bring back.
- To give back.
- To return to an earlier or original condition by repairing it.
- To receive back more than has been lost, to the point where the final state is greater than the original condition.
- Compensating after one has suffered loss.

Christ on Restoration

This is aptly demonstrated by Christ in the three parables He gave in Luke 15 concerning the lost coin, lost sheep, and lost son. The value attached to the coin and the sheep saw the owners searching diligently until it was found. Restoration implies a plan of action suitably geared toward recovery. Jesus makes it clear that no effort would be spared to ensure the restoration of the lost based on the assignment of the son of man "to seek and to save that which was lost" (see Luke 19:10).

Loss can be incurred because of carelessness, rebellion, and transgression. In the case of the lost son, he was allowed ample time and opportunity to weigh and assess his life when stricken by misfortune. It is important to note that his restoration was based on a change of mind, followed by a commitment to the father. The father was prepared to receive the lost son and kept expecting him to return.

Restoration is an integral part of God's plan.

From the very fall of man in the Garden of Eden, we see God stating His recovery plan. Scriptures clearly teach that God is intent on missions, and we are called to partner and co-labour with Him in this cause.

And I will cause hostility between you and the woman, and between your offspring and her offspring. He will strike your head, and you will strike his heel. (Genesis 3:15 - NLT).

God revealed and made Himself available so there could be a restoration of relationship between Himself and humanity. God wants humanity to be brought back into favour with Himself, where the fellowship and communion that was lost in Eden is restored through Christ. This timeless message of restoration is God's plan for all ages and all people.

This means that anyone who belongs to Christ has become a new person. The old life is gone; a new life has begun! And all of this is a gift from God, who brought us back to himself through Christ. And God has given us this task of reconciling people to him. For God was in Christ, reconciling the world to himself, no longer counting people's sins against them. And he gave us this wonderful message of reconciliation. So we are Christ's ambassadors; God is making his appeal through us. We speak for Christ when we plead, "Come back to God!" (2 Corinthians 5:17-20 – NLT).

Reconciliation and restoration are God's initiative. God's redemptive plan was wrapped up in the sacrifice of His Son, Jesus Christ, who became the propitiation for our sins. By a

121

single sacrificial offering of Jesus Christ, eternal redemption was procured. The enmity and estrangement that came through transgression were atoned for through the death of Jesus Christ.

It is important that we see God, not as one intent on punishing, but one who strives for the world to be reconciled to Him through receiving this wonderful message of hope called the gospel.

Not only have believers received and benefited from the message of reconciliation, but they have been given the responsibility of proclaiming this message. The work of Christ to the world is being completed through our witness and message. This Jesus is incessantly making His appeal through us to others concerning the need for reconciliation. We therefore speak on Christ's behalf to a lost world that salvation is in the person and work of Jesus.

Reconciled to God

You were dead because of your sins and because your sinful nature was not yet cut away. Then God made you alive with Christ, for he forgave all our sins. He canceled the record of the charges against us and took it away by nailing it to the cross. In this way, he disarmed the spiritual rulers and authorities. He shamed them publicly by his victory over them on the cross. (Colossians 2:13-15 - NLT).

It is amazing the extent to which God went to offer us our freedom from the very things that held us in bondage. We bask in the freedom He offers, knowing it came at a heavy price. Not only did He make us alive who were dead in trespasses and sins, but the record of charges against us was cancelled. This means we are justified simply by accepting the finished work. The cross that was a show of humiliation became the hope of our redemption. This sacrifice of Christ won a public victory as it disarmed spiritual rulers and authorities. Access is now granted to all who will acknowledge what Christ has done and receive Him as their only Lord and Saviour.

All barriers that isolated us have now been removed, and we are no longer under condemnation because of our relationship with Christ. Instead of a curse, the believers are now blessed by God through Jesus Christ (see Ephesians 1:3).

It is important for us to understand that God has made possible a way of escape for us. We are no more alienated from Him through evil thoughts and actions but have now been brought into His very presence to share in communion with Him. We therefore stand blameless before Him because of what Christ has done.

For God in all his fullness was pleased to live in Christ, and through him God reconciled everything to himself. He made peace with everything in heaven and on earth by means of Christ's blood on the cross. This includes you who were once far away from God. You were his enemies, separated from him by your evil thoughts and actions. Yet now he has reconciled you to himself through the death of Christ in his physical body. As a result, he has brought you into his own presence, and you are holy and blameless as you stand before him without a single fault. (Colossians 1:19-22 - NLT).

The message of reconciliation is a message of peace, hope, and goodwill. God's intention is clearly stated and articulated that all men everywhere are one in Him. This is the power of reconciliation that silences prejudices, biases, and all manner of hostilities. We are all a part of God's wonderful family with equal rights and privileges.

Together as one body, Christ reconciled both groups to God by means of his death on the cross, and our hostility toward each other was put to death. He brought this Good News of peace to you Gentiles who were far away from him, and peace to the Jews who were near. Now all of us can come to the Father through the same Holy Spirit because of what Christ has done for us. So now you Gentiles are no longer strangers and foreigners. You are citizens along with all of God's holy people. You are members of God's family. (Ephesians 2:16-19 - NLT).

Restoration Relationship

The least challenging thing to do would be to walk away rather than endeavour to restore others to fellowship when we consider their transgression. We can be found guilty sometimes of protecting the image of the organisation at the expense of helping those needing restoration. The two unique qualities of passion and compassion are needed in all aspects of interpersonal relationships. We must love enough to forgive but also discipline (not punish). Correction must never be done out of hate, spite, or resentment but with a view of helping to restore to fellowship.

Jesus's treatment of both the woman caught in the act of adultery (see John 8:3-11), and the woman that they called a sinner (see Luke 7:39) is very instructive. While not condoning their sinful proclivities, He offered and extended mercy and forgiveness. God is not on a mission to condemn and destroy but rather to restore. Everyone has a past and a history of failings and failures. We were never meant to be condemned to that state but rather we have the reassurances, through God's Word, that we can be delivered. Christ came to reconcile the two extremes of justice and mercy through Him becoming the propitiation for all sins. We who have received mercy must show ourselves merciful.

Jesus clearly stated that offenses would come (see Luke 17:1); in other words, it is inevitable. Personal differences and perspectives have a way of challenging interpersonal relationships. How we manage our emotions and dealings with others will determine the outcome. Offense is indeed the greatest relationship destroyer.

Scriptures clearly teach reconciliation, even if your brother has a cause against you, whether justifiably or not (see Matthew 5:23-24). Reconciliation is always far more important than simply the observance of religious duty. No matter how fervent our service is to God, poor interpersonal relationships will never be endorsed. We are also encouraged by Apostle Paul to live peaceably with others.

Do all that you can to live in peace with everyone. (Romans 12:18 - NLT).

The temptation to retaliate in like mind or make the transgressor serve a worse fate is always a challenge. The Bible however is clear procedurally how such matters should be handled when a believer sins against another. Correction must be done in love and in the spirit of reconciliation and restoration.

If another believer sins against you, go privately and point out the offense. If the other person listens and confesses it, you have won that person back. But if you are unsuccessful, take one or two others with you and go back again, so that everything you say may be confirmed by two or three witnesses. If the person still refuses to listen, take your case to the church. Then if he or she won't accept the church's decision, treat that person as a pagan or a corrupt tax collector. (Matthew 18:15-17 – NLT).

- The instruction is to first go privately and point out the area of the offense. If the person is willing to listen and confess to the wrong, then fellowship is restored as the offender repents.

- If the initial approach is unsuccessful, then two other witnesses should be taken to provide another opportunity at restoration.
- If there is still a blunt refusal on the offenders' part, then the matter should be taken to the church for a resolution. If the advice of the church is not heeded, then the one transgressing would have broken fellowship.

The best way to solve a problem is to avert one. Falling victim to the temptation to sin is quite a challenge to the believing community. There will be times when a loving but firm reprimand in correcting the offender will serve as a reminder of God's standards to all. We are further admonished to be impartial in how we deal with erring members. Reverence for God can serve as a deterrent to engaging in sinful practices.

Those who sin should be reprimanded in front of the whole church; this will serve as a strong warning to others. I solemnly command you in the presence of God and Christ Jesus and the highest angels to obey these instructions without taking sides or showing favoritism to anyone. Never be in a hurry about appointing a church leader. Do not share in the sins of others. Keep yourself pure. (1 Timothy 5:20-22 - NLT).

The backdrop to this scripture was to deal with the problem of incest in the church. This presumptuous sinning resulted in a sharp rebuke so others would fear and be discouraged from the practice. It could not be left unattended and so run the risk of causing others to be emboldened in habitual sinning. All overt violations of God's law must be dealt with lovingly and decisively.

Not Rejection But Restoration

The church, as a community, has a responsibility to make restoration a priority. Galatians 6:1-2 provides a useful guide with respect to restoring someone who has been overcome by sin.

The believer who is overtaken by a fault is not one who practices sin but one who, through ignorance or inattention, has fallen prey to temptation surprisingly. This unexpected failing was not because the person is not a true Christian, but they had a temporary lapse in judgment and so slipped.

In this case, the individual's passions or temptations has gotten the better of them, resulting in them falling back into legal bondage to sin. This is not the open or scandalous and deliberate form of sinning. Sin has caused the individual to stumble before they could get away. Once the practice is discovered, then the church has a responsibility to lovingly correct and counsel the individual in the hope of restoration.

How we approach the fallen is important. These persons are normally overtly sensitive and embarrassed at the failure. They may not want to return and reunite in fellowship, preferring isolation. In our approach, the aim is not to lose them. The failure may have caused much damage to the name of Christ and His church, but we must approach with much compassion and not anger and resentment.

The admonition to restore must be carried out by spiritual and not carnal Christians. These are Christians who have received and are being led by the Holy Spirit. They know the ways of God and have deep spiritual habits and devotion, having undergone spiritual formation. They are Christ-like and exemplary examples of Christian conduct and behaviour, clearly demonstrating the fruit of the Spirit. They are mediators not meddlers who would make matters worse. The focus would be on restoration rather than punishment, not being so enraged by the offense that they are blinded to the need for help. In some instances, it is easier to cut off than restore, accepting no responsibility to help but blaming the offender because we cannot deal with the offense of the sin. The aim of the spiritual person would be to restore men to God and to fellowship with the church.

It is clear, as evidenced from the Parable of the Samaritan (see Luke 10:25-37), that titles, for example, Priest and Levite, do not equip you to restore. Your position in church does not mean you are spiritual. It is possible to be working for God yet not doing His works. In dealing with the fallen, we need caregivers and not gravediggers. Spiritual believers must attend to the issue of restoration in dealing with the sinning brother.

Restoration will involve correction with no feeling of resentment or thoughts of punishment. It is a term associated with the mending of nets or a medical term for setting a

129

dislocated limb. In restoration, there is no pretending that the sin never happened or punishing the offender too harshly. Restoration must never be associated with victimisation. In restoration, the offender needs to be protected from other potentially explosive situations. The covering is so the individual can be helped while healing. We therefore partner with God to help the member to become whole and functional again.

Restoration can also be done through reproof, instruction, and exhortation so the member can recover from faults and errors. The task of restoration is extremely delicate and must be approached with much prayer and wisdom and with the right attitude/spirit. There is the need for kindness, love, gentleness, patience, and a forgiving spirit. In restoration, the church should be far more welcoming than seeking to shun out of great concern for the welfare of the member. Care must not just be talked about, it must be shown.

We are fully aware of our own weaknesses, hence, the attitude with which we approach the fallen must not be legalistic but compassionate. It is important to guard against the issue of pride as well as the potential dangers of what the offender fell prey to. We must never get tired of doing good repeatedly. When we add value to the lives of others, we are living the message of restoration and causing impact at the same time.

Conclusion

It is the distinct pleasure of the author to have accompanied you on this journey to transformation. I am aware that the material is applicable towards your spiritual development and contains vital information that can be shared in small groups or with the general church. I ask that you be patient with yourself as the Holy Spirit continues to work on your heart and life.

Spiritual formation will take time. It requires discipline and consistency. In some instances, new habits will need to be formed to obtain the real value from this book. Read the book with a Bible on hand and a willingness to be guided by the Holy Spirit—it will be easier to apply what you have understood.

My prayer for the readers is taken from the book of Ephesians:

I pray that your hearts will be flooded with light so that you can understand the confident hope he has given to those he called—his holy people who are his rich and glorious inheritance. I also pray that you will understand the incredible greatness of God's power for us who believe him. (Ephesians 1:18-19 – NLT).

This book was written to facilitate serious introspection. As you evaluate your life according to the Word, my prayer is that life change will occur.

Coming Soon

Other Books by the Author

Printed in Great Britain
by Amazon

30237382R00076